DESTINATION WEALTH

Dear Jordan,

I trust that D.W. will inspire you to begin an amazing journey!

Dave.

3-2-23

Destination Wealth: 5 Financial Success Secrets to Make Your Money Work for You

1st Edition

Cover artwork: *Alison Du Toit*
Editor: *Joshua Lisec*
Designer: *Aimèe Armstrong*

Prepared for print by Nuance Editing & Writing.
www.nuanced.co.za

Printed and bound in South Africa
print@tandym.co.za

ISBN – 13
978-0-620-89047-2

DESTINATION WEALTH

5 Financial Success Secrets to Make Your Money
Work for You

DAVE FISHER (CFP)®

Contents

Acknowledgements

MY JOURNEY WITH *Destination Wealth* has been much like the story of the Chinese Bamboo tree which takes five years, from being planted as a seed to finally breaking the soil and growing to be a majestic 80 ft tree.

Thanks be to God for creating me with such an incredible purpose and blessing me along each step of the journey. So many amazing people planted the seed, watered it, fed it and then guided its growth.

Thanks to my wife Karen for encouraging and believing in me, along with all the hours of editing. To my supportive friend and business partner, Andrew Dugmore, thanks Dr for helping to make this possible. To Annelise de Jager, for regular progress checks, 'gentle' nudges and for sharing your inspiring story.

To my friends and clients who identified and awakened the seed and who trusted and believed in me. My long-term friend and client, Jerry Novak, deserves special mention in this regard.

To Nick Binnedell, Fabien Durocher-Yvon, Shireen Chengadu, Karl Hofmeyr, Dean Davey, Nicky Perdijk, Nhlamulo Ngobeni, Wally and Glenda Morehen and so many others for sharing your stories.

To all who supported me in this endeavour, including Fisher Dugmore team members Louisa Grobler, Ciska Giacometti-Smith, Theresa Swart and Claudette Koeleman. Special thanks to my friend and associate,

Tyrone Peddie, for your input. To Kerri Girnun, Marius van der Merwe and Bianca Keyser for your feedback and encouragement, and to Alison du Toit for your creative input in the cover design.

Last but definitely not least, to Joshua Lisec, Nadja Botha and Saskia Brits for pruning and shaping the final stages of this book's growth.

Foreword

Jeanette Marais, Deputy CEO of Momentum Metropolitan

ONE OF MY GREATEST passions in life is to open up the world of finances to people from all walks of life. To me, it is important that everyone understands that a few good habits and a basic understanding of key concepts can put you well on your way to financial success.

Personal finance is not just about numbers and money. It is about people's hopes, fears and dreams. It actually is just that – personal and unique. Contrary to how people tend to look at their own finances, and how they think of themselves as rational, this is not a cold rational topic, but a highly emotional part of everyone's life.

Add complexity to an emotive topic, and people tend to become even wearier of the conversation. One of my sisters is a doctor, an intelligent woman, but she knows little about financial services or the jargon that is so often used in the industry. If I read or edit a financial services article or brochure, I often ask her what she understands of the content. And more often than not it's hard to understand and too complex.

The complexity in financial services is usually not because clients aren't smart enough or uneducated. It might be that they are not interested (yet...), that money is not top of mind or that the topic is too sensitive. We as professionals in the industry have a duty to make personal finance clear, understandable and interesting, so that people are able to prioritise it in their lives.

As part of opening up the world of financial services, this book breaks down some of the complexity. Therefore, I am honoured to write the foreword to a book written by a financial adviser of the highest integrity, one that I have known for many years – Dave Fisher.

What better way is there to bring concepts across than storytelling, which Dave does very well. The stories in this book are real-life examples of Dave's clients with whom you can identify and find inspiration from. To be honest, after reading the book, I was almost jealous; I wished I had written this.

I agree with Dave that our ability to achieve financial success is closely linked to our financial context – our money mindset. My personal finance story began while growing up on a farm in the Free State. My dad was a farmer, and my mom a teacher with a university degree – quite an achievement in the late sixties. When she met and fell in love with my father, she gave up her career and salary to get married and raise five kids.

I have childhood memories of waking up at night, hearing my mom and dad argue about money. I realised later that it had little to do with money – it was all about my mom's struggle with her own identity, and being dependent on my father for money to run the household. This is one example of a deep human need that is inextricably linked to finances: to be empowered and in control of your own life, you need money.

And after realising the predicament my mom was in, I knew from a young age that I wanted to be financially independent and successful in my own right. I vowed that I would never be in the same position she was, and I always knew that I had to maintain my own identity and manage my own finances, and I still do. Basically, I realised at a young age that 'a man is not a financial plan'.

We often don't acknowledge the role that money plays in our identity.

My own passion for financial literacy has been growing over the years.

One of the pivotal moments was when the husband of someone close to me passed away at 40. Both of them earned a salary and they were equal breadwinners, but she left the managing of the finances to her husband. She thought that they were financially sound, which was very far from the truth. I was glad that I could step in with my background and experience to help the family. But what if she did not have the support? She would've lost everything, and this while she thought they were fine.

Women often think that their husband or partner would provide for them. Not only is it empowering to know what is going on in your finances, it also makes the future exciting. You can plan for and live your dream.

Dave and his business partner, Andrew Dugmore, were early adopters who knew how an investment platform could benefit their clients when my team launched one of the very first investment platforms in the country, called Momentum Administration Services, in 1995. This business has subsequently grown to a business with billions of assets under management. In those days there were only 39 unit trusts. Today there are more than 2 000. Dave always had an investment mindset with the aim of helping his clients. If his clients were successful, Dave knew that he would be successful, so his focus was never on himself, but on the needs of his clients. Dave shares with us his 'success secrets', but don't be fooled. This isn't quick tips on how to 'get rich'.

To build and protect wealth, financially successful people stick with a long-term strategy aimed at achieving long-term financial goals. This is one of the many touch points in our lives and in the book that I identify with.

The value of financial advice cannot be highlighted enough. Dave makes you excited to have a financial planner and the value that he adds to his clients in a practical manner gives them a future to look forward to while still being comfortable in the present.

Every person's context is different and you shouldn't compare yourself with other people to determine if you're successful or not. Each person's financial plan will look different. If you are doing what you want to do and make your money work for you personally, you will be successful. If you want to live a fulfilled life, you need to get perfect alignment with your reason for being. Ask yourself why *you* are on Earth? Then match your financial context and your lifestyle with this purpose and you will be forever grateful.

The 'success secrets' that Dave shares in this book are important steps you can take to change your thinking about what wealth means, to think about your long-term financial goals and the practical steps to ultimately reach those goals.

Dave, I can see that your heart is in this book and it is the culmination of years of experience in the financial services world and providing clients with valuable financial advice. This book is not another textbook about money. It was written with energy, it is highly personal and it reads like a story. Thank you for the role you play in enabling people – not just to understand finances, but to achieve their goals and purposefully live their dreams.

INTRODUCTION

From Penniless to Prosperous

I met Dave Fisher in 2002. He has been my financial coach and great friend ever since. Dave coached me on wealth and money issues, and we put a financial plan together. In the beginning of our relationship, Dave must have been pulling his hair out at my ill-discipline. But he's been patient and consistent, and, thanks largely to him, I am in a blessed financial situation today.

– Dean Raymond Davey, executive director, Workforce Advisory

IN MY THIRTY YEARS of experience as a financial planner, I have dealt with thousands of individuals from all walks of life. What struck me most is how closely our ability to achieve financial success is linked to our financial context – our money mindset. We explore this further in the next chapter.

A strong motivator for writing this book is that so many individuals, regardless of their academic intelligence, effort or even income, tend to achieve no greater financial success than their parents or peer groups. My purpose is to teach you how to change your context to achieve success in all areas of your life. Allow me to share my story.

We all experience both pain and pleasure in life. Every decision we make is either to gain pleasure or to avoid pain. Pain motivated me to succeed. I was the middle child among three boys. As a toddler, I struggled to learn to walk due to one leg being shorter than the other. Though I did learn to walk before the age of two, I never had the athletic ability that my brothers had. I always felt that I was the odd one out. In my teenage years, I experienced rapid physical growth, and I grew extremely tall and thin. My scrawny physique, on top of a poor self-image from childhood, drove me to change. At age sixteen, I started working out. At the time, I measured approximately 1.80 meters (m) and tipped the scales at around 70 kilograms (kg). Driven by my desire to improve, I spent many hours at the gym. By age twenty-three, I weighed over 130 kg and stood 2.03 meters (m) tall. I loved how it felt to exhaust my muscles and to watch my body reap the benefits. I learned self-discipline, which helped me succeed in other areas of life.

My father had a successful career in marketing and worked himself up the corporate ladder to eventually become the company's marketing director. We lived a comfortable life on his salary. Unfortunately, however, I grew up with a lot of criticism from my father, which further fuelled my determination to succeed.

After leaving university and completing my national service, I met my first wife. The marriage failed early, leaving me with more debt than I could manage. Before I knew it, I was on the verge of losing my business, my home and my car. The pain of powerlessness resurrected my teenage determination to make a change. I set savings goals and worked like a

Trojan to repay my debt. That began my journey to financial success. I threw myself wholeheartedly into my business, read books fervently, attended courses and seminars and met friends, clients and associates who shaped my trajectory.

I must admit that young Dave had a very different image of the future than where life took him. As a kid, I assumed I would become a lawyer, but I did not give much thought to my purpose – why I was put on Earth in the first place. I grew up in a Christian home, but, apart from baptism as a baby, confirmation as a teenager and the occasional church service, my faith was academic and shallow. After meeting and marrying Karen, the love of my life, I started attending church regularly and was blessed to meet special people and attend events, such as the Walk to Emmaus and Angus Buchan's Mighty Men Conference. Looking back, I see how Jeremiah 1:5 has come true for me. The verse reads, "Before I formed you in the womb I knew you, and before you were born I consecrated you; I appointed you a prophet to the nations" (ESV).

If you are not a person of faith, perhaps you can appreciate Mark Twain's sentiment that "the two most important days in your life are the day you are born and the day you find out why". I believe that everything that happens in life points us towards our sense of purpose. I have discovered that my purpose – my *why*, as TED-speaker Simon Sinek puts it – is to help others find theirs to become the best version of themselves and planning their financial affairs accordingly. I was able to fulfil this purpose because I have achieved it myself.

With blessings from above, through determination and supportive mentorships and because of prudent financial decisions, I have been able to build wealth beyond anything I had ever imagined possible. My now significant and steadily growing investments are housed in various trusts, companies, properties and equities. This achievement has afforded my family and I the opportunity to live a lifestyle that has included international holidays and other memorable experiences that I had never thought possible when I was growing up.

Today, through our financial services group of companies, the Fisher Dugmore Group, we advise, coach and mentor other South Africans to achieve the success they desire too. Together with my business partner,

Andrew Dugmore, and our hand-picked team of financial planners, we teach clients to implement smart, sustainable financial plans that enable them to live their ideal lifestyle. Much credit goes to Andrew for the financial success secrets revealed in this book. We have learned much from each other over the past twenty years. He too has a story of pain, change and achievement.

Andrew was born into an ordinary, middle-class family. His father was an ordained Methodist minister, and his mother was a nursing tutor. His dad earned a moderate income of around R 160 to R 200 per month. His parents had never owned a home until he was sixteen. Andrew's mother instilled in him the belief that every cloud has a silver lining. She worked two jobs, day and night, to make ends meet and to be able to afford private tuition and horse-riding lessons for Andrew and his brother.

The private schools that Andrew had attended introduced him to children with wealthy parents. Their lifestyle appealed to him, so he decided to improve his financial circumstances and earn his own money. Andrew's ambitions took him from growing and selling vegetables as a youngster to a number of part-time jobs in the six months between graduating from university and beginning his two years of national service. He learned many valuable lessons in this time, mostly that he didn't wish to deal with complaints all day and that he wanted to be his own boss.

A turning point in Andrew's career arrived when a friend offered him an opportunity to join his sales team selling Reeva Forman cosmetics, with the promise of big earnings. Still desiring the wealth of his childhood friends' families, he jumped at the opportunity. The sales job came with a condition – all Reeva Forman salespeople had to pay for a week-long training session, or they were out. The training turned out to be a major catalyst in his life. Reeva Forman, a formidable woman with not a single negative word in her vocabulary, made Andrew and other trainees believe that right thinking and hard work could accomplish impossible tasks. His cosmetics sales journey took him all over Pretoria and later to Johannesburg and the Witwatersrand. Orders grew so large that Andrew eventually employed students to deliver them!

Right through his two years of compulsory military service, Andrew worked. While other airmen and women spent evenings in bars, Andrew walked the streets with his briefcase. During one delivery run, he met Dr. Reg Barrett from the Theosophical Society, an ancient order dedicated to cultivating spiritual wisdom. That chance meeting blossomed into a mentorship. Dr. Barrett taught Andrew many important financial stewardship truths, including that money only stays with you if you share it with worthy causes; money is only paper and numbers – it is a means to an end; spend money wisely; and save up for a rainy day.

Andrew brought many of these lessons to the Fisher Dugmore Group. For example, we teach every client how to build up an emergency fund to weather life's storms, from pandemics to retrenchment – a panic fund, as one staff member calls it. You will learn this and other practical financial planning steps (and begin to take them) in the forthcoming chapters.

Broadly speaking, *Destination Wealth* is the culmination of my and Andrew's personal experiences and professional financial advising careers. We are driven by our shared passion to help others make changes to live up to their financial potential. In this book, I apply modern psychology to money management in order to answer South Africans' most pressing questions about earning, budgeting, saving, spending and investing. It is a collection of never-before-seen-publicly financial planning insights, which offers a proven process to build and protect wealth at any age and income, through simple mindset shifts and sustainable behaviour changes. In this book, I show you how to upgrade the way that you think about money so that you can earn (and keep) more of it, protect your most important asset (it's not what you think!) and multiply meagre savings into a remarkable fortune, and much, much more. It's all legal, all ethical and all for South African professionals, students, families and pensioners.

Now, why do I focus on South Africa? Because many books have been written on general financial planning principles for people of any background. But, just as every nation has its own language and culture so does every country have its own laws, regulations and taxes. It is my desire for this book to help all my fellow South Africans navigate these rules and make wise financial decisions that ultimately usher in a new era of prosperity – a golden age for our country.

If you watch the local news, you realise how much we need such a transformation. South Africa has experienced a difficult political history, resulting in extreme unemployment. Nearly half of us live below the poverty line. We have low levels of national savings, which burdens the state, forcing our government to borrow more and more money to keep up with welfare payments as we retire and reach old age. According to the National Treasury, only six percent of South Africans are on track to retire comfortably.[1] The rest of us are expected to rely on public funds through taxation or through charitable giving, neither of which is sustainable for our fast-growing population.

South Africa's current economic environment has left many feeling hopeless, negative and stuck in survival mode. The COVID-19 pandemic has only made matters worse. South Africa's economy collapsed along with that of the world. It was far from good. Two separate healthcare systems, one private for the well-off and one public for everyone else, further damaged trust in our government. Some say it's better to leave these shores and live somewhere far away, perhaps in the United States, Canada or New Zealand. Your money will fare better, and your health probably will too, claim the naysayers.

Whatever your thoughts, the fact is, we need change. But massive transformation at a societal level can be made only at the individual level, not from the top-down. If South Africa is to achieve prosperity for all, then *all* of us must change. We must change how we save money, how we spend money, how we budget, how we invest, and, mostly, how we *think* about money, which is why the beginning sections of this book are dedicated to the mental game of money – your financial context.

One of the world's best known and respected investors and fourth wealthiest man in the world Warren Buffet once said, "Only when the tide goes out you discover who has been swimming naked". Although he was referring to those who take undue risks when investing, I feel that the prevailing crises have highlighted the inadequate and even poor financial planning in many people's financial lives, which leaves them exposed and vulnerable.

---

1   Jooste, R. (2019). 'Most South Africans Will Face a Bleak Reality When Their Working Lives Comes to an End'. *Business Maverick*. September 9, 2019. Available at: https://www.dailymaverick.co.za/article/2019-09-09-most-south-africans-will-face-a-bleak-reality-when-their-working-lives-come-to-an-end.

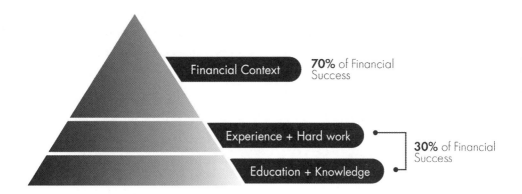

Figure 1. Context – the catalyst for success

When we as a nation follow the five steps detailed in this book, our people will stop merely surviving and start thriving. We will renew hope in every home across our land. Industriousness will rise as taxes fall. As more and more citizens invest, we will become more entrepreneurial. We will focus on opportunities rather than on risks. We will feel encouraged, not threatened. We will help each other discover our passions, turn them into businesses and live out our dreams together. Through entrepreneurs opening businesses, more respectable, well-paying jobs will be created. More jobs mean more money for people to invest in the nation. These investments will uplift the entire economy.

In the same way that the mass adoption of the principles in *Destination Wealth* will benefit South Africa, so too will they benefit you personally. At the time of writing this, it is clear that you will only be able to provide for yourself and your family upon your death in a meaningful way through your own wise money management. The government surely isn't able to. Either you do it or you and those you love will be in serious trouble.

Personally, I am cautiously optimistic about the prospects for South Africa. The before-and-after financial conditions that we see every day in Fisher Dugmore clients' lives are like green shoots appearing all across a sun-baked savannah. Great things are ahead. At the same time, we are realistic. There is much progress to be made. That's the reason I tell all clients – and why I now tell you – to think of yourself as a global citizen. We must be shrewd about where and how to invest within our borders, while opening our minds to (and spreading our buckets among) offshore investment opportunities. I delve into both concepts later on in this book.

For now, I want to affirm your commitment to South Africa. Yes, we have problems. Yes, they require solutions. But if you are positive about South Africa's prospects, you will be able to create a difference in your life, in your family's lives and in many other lives in our nation. In the pages ahead, I teach you how.

So begins your journey to Destination Wealth.

FINANCIAL PLANNING SUCCESS SECRET #1:

Upgrade Your Financial Context

In working with Dave through the years, he must have said a thousand times, "Your money is not working for you. You should leverage your money better". Thanks to him, I finally got it. I am extremely thankful for the fact that I was able to support both my parents financially as they grew older. This would not have been possible had I not developed my own thinking about money and gotten the best advice from my friend and wealth mentor over many years. Lesson learned: listen to Dave.

– Annelise de Jager, entrepreneur and inspirational teacher

Why We're All So Weird about Money

HAVE YOU EVER WONDERED why some high-earners can't make their bond payments? Why do many successful actors, athletes and artists retire into bankruptcy? Why does a simple budget feel like a life-or-death struggle?

The answer is one and the same. Throughout my career as a financial planner working with thousands of individuals, couples and families from all walks of life, I've discovered this answer. Before Fisher Dugmore Group clients and I ever talk about investments, asset classes or tax planning strategies, we lay the foundation for their financial success. How? We upgrade their financial context. Like a smart speaker that controls every device in your home, your financial context answers every question you'll ever ask about money – whether you realise it or not.

Financial context: The idea that our financial decisions derive from our accumulated beliefs about and emotions around wealth, ultimately determining how much money we can or can't have.

Your financial context explains every money decision that you've ever made or ever will make – to budget or not to budget, to invest or not to invest and so forth. Our financial context sets the stage for the level of wealth that we're comfortable with and are able to attain and, more importantly, what level of wealth we keep. When I meet with clients, I often refer to financial context as a 'money muscle', as its strength determines whether you can achieve your financial goals.

For example, if your financial context is *big*, you believe in abundance. You focus on the long term. You feel positive towards others. You're a giver, not a taker, and this only seems to increase your savings. People who follow the path of abundance tend to live life to the fullest.

If you have a *small* financial context, you're the opposite. There's simply not enough to go around. You blame someone else for your financial woes, whether that be the government, the taxman, your employer, your financial adviser, your parents or your spouse. This scarcity tends to go hand-in-hand with sadness, jealousy and gambling addictions. Strangely, these people believe in money for nothing – that money will manifest out of thin air. Many people have a small financial context. The average American household spends $1 000 a year on lottery tickets, even though they're 251 times more likely to be hit by lightning than to win.

Someone with a small financial context is probably poor at financial planning. When this person experiences an unexpected financial event, they instinctively have a fight-or-flight response, similar to our prehistoric ancestors when being attacked by a sabre-toothed tiger. Though our ancestors' fight-or-flight response may have ensured survival, a similar response to a financial crisis does nothing to help the situation. Suppose a medical emergency befalls a family during the weekend. This family has little in savings, so they have to charge the hospital bill on a high-interest credit card. Their income doesn't cover the minimum monthly payments, which damages their credit score. They've limited their own ability to buy a car, a house and more.

Have you heard of the Matthew effect? It takes its name from the words of Jesus in Matthew 13:12: "Whoever has will be given more, and they will have an abundance. Whoever does not have, even what they have will be taken from him" (NIV). The big financial context of abundance versus the small financial context of scarcity perfectly illustrates the Matthew effect.

If you feel that you relate more to the small financial context, not to worry. It *is* possible to expand your financial context, be mindful about money, feel more relaxed and enter a state of abundance. Abundant thinking combined with good financial planning result in lifestyle sustainability. It also allows us to be prepared for or equipped to deal with unexpected events, such as being laid off, a decline in business, medical bills, car maintenance and even having to travel to attend a wedding or funeral. You behave more rationally with money, no matter what life throws your way.

However, you don't need to 'fix' your financial context. It's not broken. There is no right or wrong financial context, nor is there one that is 100 percent abundance or 100 percent scarcity. In fact, there's a wide range that I consider to be healthy. Unfortunately, most of us aren't in that range. The most common reason is that we tend to live lifestyles beyond our means. We're then unable to prioritise financial planning, and our families tend to pay the price somewhere down the line. Globally, a combination of poor financial planning and increased longevity are pointing to a scary financial future. This is highlighted in these South African retirement statistics:

- 91 percent will be forced to continue working, depend on state welfare or rely on family support.
- Only nine percent will be financially independent or comfortably well-off.

Contrary to what most people think, it's easier to increase your financial context than to decrease your lifestyle. What's important right now is that we understand how our financial context developed. Then we can evaluate whether it serves our purpose and, if necessary, change it. Once you understand how your financial context had developed in your formative years, you'll learn how to take control of your finances.

So, You Have a Financial Context. Where Did It Come From?

Few people ever realise that they *have* a financial context, much less that it's possible to transform it. Where does our financial context come from? Our upbringing, our parents, our peers and their beliefs about money are our most influential context shapers. In other words, *luck* determines our financial context. You don't get to choose where you're born or where you live as a child. You don't get to choose your parents' financial history or who you go to school with. Our family and social circle influence our beliefs and behaviours, playing a significant role in how we spend and save years later.

Have you ever noticed that most people tend to emulate the financial results of their parents and peers? Regardless of their education, intelligence, effort and even income, they fail to achieve financial success beyond what they know – even if they know better. When people acquire more wealth than their financial context has prepared them for, they cannot help but sabotage themselves. That's why about 70 percent of lottery winners lose all their winnings in five years or less.[2] Why does this happen? Usually, gamblers grow up in a family of gamblers. Mum had always said that she'd win the lottery one day. Friends at school gambled. You couldn't escape it. And you most likely didn't want to. In the early 1990s, Italian scientists discovered neurons in our brains that fire not only when we perform an action but also when we observe others performing that same action. The scientists named these 'mirror neurons' because they cause us to mirror other people's actions. We don't need a study to know this is true. Babies, older children and even young adults learn through the process of mirroring others. Monkey see, monkey do. This explains why most people tend to emulate their parents and peers in the way they work with money.

This also explains why learned helplessness is common in humans. This was discovered by Martin Seligman, the founding father of positive psychology. When we fail or see others fail, we can become so hopeless that we simply give up. This is why poverty is often perpetuated from one generation to the next. A scarcity context tends to become a self-fulfilling prophecy.

Thinking and acting like those who raised us isn't always intentional. Nor does peer pressure always take the form of direct encouragement. Many people go along with their family's or group's behaviour without even realising they're doing it. Therefore, if your social environment (friends, colleagues, teammates, etc.) has a poor financial context, you'll likely adopt one too. It's difficult to elevate yourself above your peer group. It's only human to want to be accepted by a group. If your friends spent money that they didn't have, you probably felt like you were expected to do the same. If your parents lived beyond their means, your financial context as an overspender was set.

In short, you can accurately say that every money decision that you've made up to this point in your life is not entirely your fault.

---

2   Crouch, M. (2020). '13 Things Lotto Winners Won't Tell You: Life after Winning the Lottery'. *Reader's Digest*. January 24, 2020 (updated). Available at: https://www.rd.com/advice/saving-money/13-things-lottery-winners.

The way your parents and peers talked about and used money has shaped your attitudes and habits, forming your current financial context.

A Path to Financial Success

Every human heart longs for prosperity, but seldom does our financial context set us on a path that leads to success. What do I mean by success?

Success: Accomplishment of a purpose.

This is the broadest dictionary definition of success. But there are as many personal definitions of success as there are people on Earth. Success can be emotional, i.e. contentment. Success can be intellectual, i.e. intelligence. Success can be spiritual, i.e. enlightenment. And of course, success can be financial, i.e. wealth. Our financial success (or lack thereof) affects these other key areas of life. How we live, who we marry, where we worship, how we communicate, which car we drive, what food we eat, where we work and more are all influenced by how much money we have, or don't have.

What about success on a basic human level? If you're familiar with world-renowned coach and speaker Tony Robbins, you may have heard him speak about the six core human needs:

1. Certainty: The need for security, stability and reliability.
2. Uncertainty: The need for variety and challenges.
3. Significance: The need to feel important, needed, wanted and worthy of love.
4. Love and connection: The need to feel connected with and loved by other human beings.
5. Growth: The need for constant development emotionally, intellectually and spiritually.
6. Contribution: The need to give beyond ourselves to others.

What do these needs have to do with financial success? Although money isn't one of our core needs, it does play a starring role in all six. For example, we can't achieve certainty without money to provide for food and shelter. We can't focus on personal growth if we're worrying about paying bills. And we certainly can't help others if we can't provide for ourselves.

Is financial success the key to complete fulfilment? Yes and no. People think more money will make them happier. However, money only buys happiness up to a certain point – the point that it secures the material necessities in life, starting with food, clothes and shelter. No matter how much money you have, you must support your family's chosen lifestyle. That's why I always tell my financial planning clients that to understand your personal financial circumstances is to lay the foundation to achieve financial sustainability.

Our parents and grandparents often attribute financial success to academic achievement. Academic ability usually means career success and a higher income. Think of fields such as medicine, law, accounting and engineering. Usually, career success, and the higher income that comes with it, is the result of knowledge, experience and work ethic.

Although intelligence plays a significant role in how much money we *earn*, our financial context determines how much money we *keep*. While academic education focuses on teaching the conscious mind, modern neuroscience has revealed that 95 percent of our brain activity is subconscious. If our environment, our beliefs and our resulting behaviours facilitate wealth building, guess what we'll do? Build wealth. Financial decisions that protect your assets, grow your investments and safeguard your legacy become as innate as breathing. You can't *help* but get rich.

What if that's not you? What if your surroundings and habits lean towards the opposite? Most of us weren't taught the financial success secrets of the one percent. Fewer still grew up around influences that ingrained wise money choices into our mindset. For example, consider Fisher Dugmore client Dean's story.

From Broke to Blessed: Dean's Story

Dean grew up in a small mining town in South Africa, where a souped-up Nissan Skyline and a two-hundred-square-metre house made you the who's-who of the town. Dean's family didn't have that. His dad worked sixteen hours a day most days to earn overtime. He would start work at 5:00 a.m., work until 3:00 p.m., then go back to work at 6:00 p.m. until midnight.

Dean's dad worked these insane hours for very little money. He often only ran into his dad as he got home from school sports, when his dad had woken up for his evening shift. He often asked his dad why he didn't leave the mine for a better-paying job. His response? Mining was all he knew how to do. Despite years in the mine, he never achieved management status.

Dean's mom worked mostly night shifts in the local hospital as a nurse. As a result, much of Dean's formative childhood was spent under the watchful eye of the family's live-in nanny. His parents' wages covered the essentials, but the family always faced financial pressure. On or around the twentieth of every month, the well was dry, as Dean's mother would say. Whenever Dean needed school or sports supplies, his mother would ask her employer for an advance against her salary to pay for them. In those days, local public school fees were low. Still, if Dean's dad missed an overtime shift, he had to dip into savings or cancel an insurance policy to afford to make ends meet. How is it that Dean's parents failed to manage their money? They didn't have a budget or a financial planner. They never talked about their money woes, and Dean didn't know that there were other ways to handle money.

When Dean turned fifteen, he asked his dad about going to university.

"There's no money for that," he told Dean. "You'll have to go to work in the mines with me to pay for it first. That or work hard for scholarships."

It's a good thing Dean excelled at sports. He earned a sports scholarship to attend the University of Pretoria, where he initially enrolled in a communications management course. The reason for Dean's choice was that his girlfriend at the time took that course. But when he arrived for the first lecture, Dean realised the entire course was in Afrikaans. Dean's parents were the children of Scottish immigrants, so he spoke English.

The first course in English that Dean found was law, so he switched to that.

He enjoyed it, so he finished the programme and graduated with a law degree. Then he decided that he didn't want to be a lawyer. Unsure of what to do next, Dean turned to his financially successful uncle for advice.

"Dean, if you don't know what you want to do with your life, at least do something that makes money and gives you options."

Dean went back to school, registered for accounting classes and became a chartered accountant (CA). And it was a good choice. He began an amazing professional career as an executive, partner and director at big firms, like Deloitte in South Africa, Moscow, London, the Netherlands and Belgium.

Dean's parents divorced when he was twenty-five. His dad remarried and still lives in Dean's childhood home. He was forced to retire from the mines at sixty, but he got a general operational management position at a private diamond company in the region. Now in his seventies, Dean's dad still works like a Trojan – at least twelve hours a day. He and his second wife live a modest life, but financial struggles followed him into his second marriage. They've remortgaged their home multiple times to pay for their lifestyle, which is not over the top. Without his current salary, their savings wouldn't keep them afloat.

After the divorce, Dean's mom worked as a live-in nurse for a wealthy family, tripling the salary that she had earned her entire adult life. Still, she had never managed to save enough to make herself financially independent. She recently moved into a retirement village where she lives hand-to-mouth. Dean contributes most of what is required to keep her afloat every month. He feels blessed to be in a position to contribute. How did he get there? Dean upgraded his financial context.

In the formative years of his career, Dean mirrored his parents' financial behaviour without even knowing it. Even though Dean earned more money than his parents had earned combined, he still had financial problems. He earned a decent salary, but he spent money faster than it came into the door. He had no financial planning acumen, no budget and no discipline. His stable career gave him easy access to loans, and riddled him with debt.

The surrounding culture also played a role in how he saw money.

Many South Africans (especially those who make loads of money) have a *laissez-faire* attitude about money. So did Dean. *You only live once. Enjoy yourself.* This sort of person made up the majority of Dean's friends and co-workers.

I met Dean when he was twenty-seven years old and worked as a clerk at Deloitte. At the time, Dean had recently married his first wife, also a CA. They'd bought their first home together with their combined salaries – a little duplex in a good neighbourhood. They had no savings or life insurance policies. They had invested with friends in fifteen properties, so they theoretically had a balance sheet. However, they had zero yield on any of them because nobody ran it like a business. They just kept buying properties, using their CA salaries for leverage with banks. With R 150 000 in credit card debt, a flashy Audi TT that they couldn't afford and a slew of bad investments, Dean and his wife needed a plan. They needed it yesterday! I began helping them to make that plan and dig themselves out of debt.

Unfortunately, my coaching couldn't save Dean's marriage. A young lifetime's worth of poor financial discipline carries over into other areas of life. I stood by Dean's side and helped him arbitrate a respectful, amicable and fair divorce settlement. After his divorce, he basically started his life over.

"What's next?" I asked Dean.

"I want to get out of this hole. Both financially and emotionally," he said. "I want to have kids someday, and I want to be a role model to them. Financial acumen is an important part of a father's role. I want to leave a legacy for my children – a safe future. And I want my finances to be vastly different from that of my parents."

"I can help," I said. "Let's get started."

First, we took stock of Dean's finances, unloaded his share of the properties and cut his reckless spending. He could have opened up an Abercrombie store with all the clothes he'd bought from them!

Dean then invested time and effort in drawing up a monthly budget, which he followed. By the time Dean met Annelies, a lovely accountant from

Belgium, he'd proven himself ready for commitment. Dean's reformed financial context matched her existing financial reality. Her mother was a pharmacist and entrepreneur, and her father was a lawyer. They had taught her a lot about money – how to make it *and* how to save it.

They dated, married and moved to her home country to raise their twins. To stay financially-aligned today, Dean's wife is CFO in their house. Because of her financial context, she has an edge on how to run their finances. Like his parents, Dean has always had trouble saying no. He didn't understand how small daily indulgences add up and ultimately ruin finances. Dean and his wife manage this by having one main account from which they pay their expenses. Dean also has a separate 'fun money' account for his own personal spending into which his wife transfers money each month. When it's gone, it's gone. It sounds crazy, but this arrangement works incredibly well for them.

Today, Dean and his wife feel truly blessed. They've forged meaningful careers, and they're present in their children's lives. They even stick to a weekly date night in spite of their busy schedules and work travels. I've helped them follow a personalised financial plan so that they can both achieve short-term lifestyle upgrade goals and build a long-term lasting legacy.

I've been Dean's financial adviser – and he, my friend – from when we met. I'm grateful to see Dean and his wife on a steady, continuous journey to financial success. He has developed financial planning habits that are opposite to those of his parents. Dean and his wife are building a beautiful forest villa and have travelled extensively. They have a solid asset base in first-world currency, and they follow a disciplined financial plan, yet they still live out their bucket lists in the present. Meanwhile, they're raising kids who understand the value of money. Dean not only upgraded his own financial context but has also changed the context for his family's next generation.

Change Your Context, Change Your Future

Dean changed his financial context and so can you. That doesn't mean it will be easy. Our beliefs about and behaviour around money are ingrained by our environment at an early age. Your subconscious mind will always try to revert to that comfort zone. Left unchanged, a financial context is so powerful that it overrides logic. Once our financial context develops, our brains constantly search for information to support it. At any time, there are two thousand bits of information available for our minds to comprehend. At best, we can digest 120 bits per second. What determines our brains' focus? Our existing financial context. We use our warped perception of reality to affirm our current beliefs. As author Anaïs Nin says, "We don't see things as they are, we see them as we are".

While your previous life experiences have influenced your present-day financial stability, your future is still up to you. Bill Gates, one of the world's wealthiest people, once said, "It's not your mistake if you were born poor, but if you die poor, it's your mistake". We all choose to believe we can or can't do something – either way, we're right. If you're willing to evaluate whether your financial context serves your purpose and change it, if necessary, I'll help you achieve financial independence, starting with five simple steps.

Five Steps to Transform Your Financial Context
Step #1: Start with a Vision

According to Simon Sinek, author of *Start with Why*, most people can tell you what they do. Some can tell you how. Few can tell you why. Truly successful people can clearly articulate their why – their vision for what they do in life.

Do you have a compelling vision for your career and your life that you can articulate? If not, don't worry. Discovering and defining your vision – your why – is the first step that I'm going to take with you to upgrade your financial context and achieve lasting financial success. We're all bound to experience storms in life, such as injuries, illness, divorce or retrenchment. During uncertain times, your vision will empower you to do what is right.

I recently had the privilege of meeting the courageous South African adventurer Joey Evans. Joey developed a love for off-road motorcycling at an early age. He competed in professional events until he broke his back in a freak racing accident at age thirty-two. A crushed spinal cord left Joey paralysed from his chest down. Doctors told him that he had a mere 10 percent chance of walking again.

Despite the odds, Joey chose the long road to recovery. His vision was to one day cross the finish line of the Dakar Rally, a gruelling vehicle race through the most brutal terrain on Earth. Through determination and the loving support of family and friends, Joey got back onto his feet. First standing, then walking, then running and eventually riding. In 2017, Joey Evans became the first South African to complete the Dakar Rally on a motorcycle.

If you can take just an ounce of Joey's grit and determination to live his dream, you can achieve your own vision and change your context. What do you want to change about your finances? Simply wanting more money is not a compelling vision. Why is having more money important to you? What do you see yourself doing once you're maintaining financial independence? Answer these questions and you'll find your vision.

Knowing your vision enables you to find perfect alignment among your purpose, context, income and lifestyle. For example, if your true calling in life is to become an aid worker in war-torn regions, but your financial context is to live like a rock star, your life would be a mess. You'd live in a state of confusion and never feel happy. An extreme example, but it makes my point – once you know your *why*, it's easier to determine *how* to get there.

Step #2: Take Stock

Once you know your vision, evaluate your current circumstances. Are you happy with what you've achieved, with what you have saved and with your income and your lifestyle, or do your finances frustrate you? Do you stress over your budget, your job or your dreams that you don't see a path to achieve? If you feel unhappy as you take stock of your life, that tells you that your financial context does not align with the person that you want to be. Remember Dean? He had a wonderful career, but his financial context kept him from achieving financial success.

I advise you to beware of optimism bias as you assess your current financial situation, that is, where you are versus where you would like to be. Optimism bias should not be confused with a positive mindset. Optimism bias refers to delaying proper financial planning and investing today because you have an unrealistic expectation of future prosperity. Regardless of how little you think you have to invest now, it's important to begin saving right away. Delaying the start of your investment journey will inevitably leave you with too little time to achieve your financial objectives. Taking stock can be a sobering experience, but if you're not honest with yourself about where you are and where you want to be, you won't be able to make changes. Answer these questions freely and honestly, and you'll be able to align your future behaviour with your present goals.

Step #3: Decide to Change

If you're not happy with the way things are, it's time to make a change. We can start to change our context simply by changing what we say to ourselves. Let's move you from a financial context of scarcity to one of abundance.

Have you changed your mind about your money or your life principles? Ever or recently? I hope you have because it indicates that you're open to learning. A learning mindset is essential for living a meaningful life and building wealth. Being stuck in existing beliefs can be detrimental. If you have strong views, when was the last time you checked those views against the latest research or your current circumstances? What do you decide when faced with the choice between changing your mind and defending your opinion? Do you need to change your mind? Be mindful about what you believe. Then choose new beliefs about yourself and about money. Whenever you're tempted to repeat negative self-talk, like "I always mess up", instead try an affirmation, like "I'm confident that I'll succeed". Swap the negative "I never have enough money" for a more positive "I'm good with money". Here are some more examples of positive money beliefs you can try:

- I live in a universe of abundance.
- I'm a magnet for success and good fortune.
- I'm grateful. I celebrate every day.

- I deserve to have abundance and prosperity.
- Wealth is a mindset. I'm gifted with an abundance mindset.
- I'm consciously happy and positive about money.
- I'm able to add value and bless others.

I believe in the power of affirmations like these. According to Proverbs 23:7, "For as he thinks in his heart, so is he" (NKJV). If your thoughts bounce from negativity to greed to sadness, you will be a negative, greedy, sad person. Likewise, the decision to change your financial context is a decision to reprogram your mindset. New input, new output. Affirmations of abundance can result in a life of abundance.

Step #4: Invest in Your Success

Most of us value family, friends, business, our church or religion, intellectual stimulation and physical activity. Where we invest our time and money represents what we value most. Wealth creation won't happen if you don't value it as well. If you do value financial independence, you'll need to invest time to get there. The choice to read this book and follow my steps shows that you value financial success.

Later in this book, you have the opportunity to draw up a financial plan that is personalised to your vision, income and goals. Just as I helped Dean and his wife stick with their plan, I show you how to exercise discipline so that you can achieve your financial goals as well.

Step #5: Mirror the Right People

According to financial adviser Derek Mills, daunting goals (like upgrading your context) are futile without activities to help you achieve them. The activity I recommend you start with is changing your circle. You cannot soar like an eagle if you hang around with the turkeys. If none of your friends have a financial context that you aspire to and you're committed to growing your context, it's time to change who you hang out with. As much as you can, try to interact with people who have a bigger financial context than you. You'll learn to mirror the way they think and act with money. Invite new people (and their ideas) into your life who can help your context grow.

No financial context changes overnight. It's a process. This book has many chapters, and is not made up of merely a page. Don't despair. Enjoy the journey. I'll show you that saving is exciting *and* purposeful. In the pages ahead, you'll learn to manage a personal financial system based on my river-and-dam analogy.

The River and the Dam: A Metaphor for Happy Living in Your New Financial Context

This metaphor comes up again and again in the success secrets that I share with you. It's the most effective way I've found to explain financial planning. You see, in the same way that water flows, so does money. Just as a dam holds water back for later use, you'll build a dam to protect your money from frivolous spending and an unsustainable lifestyle. Your context is the level of wealth you are comfortable with, so your context will determine the size of your dam. As you grow your financial context, so too will your dam grow.

The process of earning money and spending it on your lifestyle is your river. Your river – your money and how you spend it – can flow away unless obstructed. To control what happens with your river, you need a good old-fashioned budget. A well-structured budget makes sure an adequate portion of your income is accumulated in your dam – your assets, like savings and investments.

Funds that are allocated to wealth creation are held in various places by your dam to provide for short-, medium- and long-term needs. These places might include an emergency fund, an education fund, a retirement fund and even investing for aspirational goals.

Money: Your Servant or Your Master?

In all organisations' and individuals' financial affairs, there are two areas to focus on:

1. Income statement: shows all income and expenses.
2. Balance sheet: shows all assets and liabilities.

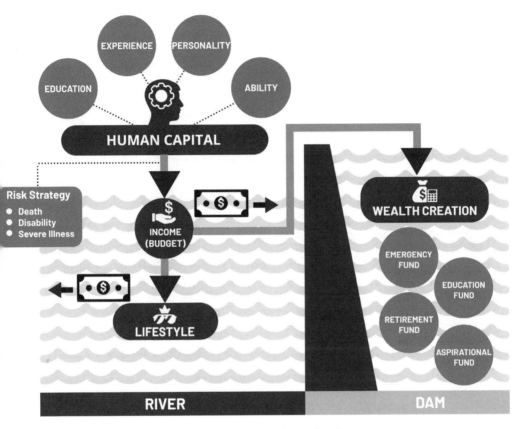

Figure 2. Financial planning – the Fisher Dugmore way

Your income statement shows your river, and your balance sheet shows your dam. In my experience, most people focus more on what's happening in the river than in the dam. If you're focused on your dam, money is your servant. If you're focused on your river, money is your master.

Dave's law on the flow of money: Money flows to the point of least resistance. If it stays in the river, it will flow away!

Financial success books often focus on earning more money. Most people believe that a big income is what makes you wealthy or prosperous and therefore constantly strive to make more money. Wanting to earn more money is not a bad thing. The problem is, if your financial planning strategy is simply to earn as much as you can and spend it, you'll become the proverbial hamster on a wheel. While it does help to earn more, if the additional cashflow doesn't result in savings, no wealth is created. The secret to wealth creation lies in consistently doing well with what you've got.

Unfortunately, peer pressure dictates that we should have homes, cars, jewellery and other material possessions to appear successful. Living an affluent lifestyle often creates a lifestyle trap – the lifestyle uses up the income and leaves little or nothing for wealth creation. Making money is only *30 percent* of wealth creation. In this regard, many professionals fall prey to the 'I've arrived'-mentality. After years of study, they finally start earning good money, then get so caught up in living an extravagant lifestyle that they never progress to the next level.

That next level is diverting income from your river into your dam to create wealth. The only effective way to control expenses in the river and to systematically allocate excess income to the dam is by having a budget and a financial plan.

Ultimately, once it achieves critical mass, your dam will become your source of income. The difference is that this income will be passive – you won't have to sell your precious time to earn it. Once the income overflow from your dam is sufficient to support your lifestyle (or has reached a growth trajectory to support your lifestyle), you can enter retirement with ease.

From Why to How

More often than not, money problems emanate from what we think and say. As pastor and author Joel Osteen says, "Whatever follows 'I am' will eventually find you. The good news is that we get to choose what follows 'I am'". I am reminded also of Proverbs 18:21a in the Bible: "Death and life are in the power of the tongue" (ESV). In life, we face problems, ranging from health to relationships to career, amongst others. In some strange way, these problems and their solutions generally impact or are impacted by our financial reality. A strong financial plan gives us the ability to overcome life's challenges more easily than it does when having a poor one. You've now laid a solid foundation for your future by making the choice to upgrade your financial context and build wealth. If this chapter is the *why*, the remaining chapters are the *how*. *How* are we going to maintain a dam that diverts enough money to live a comfortable and sustainable lifestyle? It all starts with the river – your income and your expenses. Without water, you don't have a river. You have a dried-up riverbed. And the dam doesn't exist without a river. That's why the next chapter covers how to keep your river flowing for life – how to ensure that enough money to fund your vision for your family continues to flow in every season of life, regardless of your current income level.

1. Does your financial context move you toward or away from your dreams and ambitions?
2. State your financial 'I am' in order to align with your dreams and ambitions, e.g. *I am prosperous and live a life of abundance.*

_____

_____

_____

_____

_____

_____

_____

_____

_____

_____

_____

_____

FINANCIAL PLANNING SUCCESS SECRET #2:

Protect Your Assets

I have developed an enormous amount of respect for Dave over the past thirteen years of doing business with him. His honest, sound advice regarding my income protection literally saved our livelihood and protected our future. Never in my wildest dreams did I ever think I would be medically boarded and not be able to practice dentistry anymore. And never would I have prepared financially for such a moment if I didn't have Dave's guidance. Thanks to Dave, our assets were protected. Through his humble and honest guidance, we get to live a beautiful life where I can provide for my family even without practicing my profession.

– Nicky Perdijk, PhD, dentist, entrepreneur and life coach

WHAT DO YOU FEEL when you read the following sentence?

'Living pay cheque to pay cheque.'

A little discomfort? Pulse-quickening anxiety? Stressed to the point where you would rather think about *anything* else? Whatever your reaction, I know one thing's for sure – your response to spending most, if not all, of your monthly income on expenses is *not* positive. Even if that feels natural because you grew up surrounded by people who had spent everything they had earned. Nobody wants to walk a tightrope without a safety net. That's how living pay cheque to pay cheque feels. It's like a waterfall – a river with no dam. When it's gone, it's gone. Many of South Africa's highest-salaried professionals have no safety net. What happens when the performer slips off the tightrope? If we're not able to protect our assets, we could condemn our loved ones to a life of anxiety, poverty or worse.

After Fisher Dugmore clients complete the financial context upgrade exercise, covered in Chapter 1, we shift our attention from past to future. You and I will do the same. How do we keep the river flowing today, tomorrow and for generations to come? For most people, your river is income earned from selling your time to employers or selling your talents through your own business. Your employer or customers are buying more than your time or talents. They're buying your education, experience, personality, energy, work ethic, creativity and ability. I refer to these collectively as human capital.

Human capital: The sum of your qualifications, experience, personality, work ethic and ability that enables you to earn an income from an employer or run a successful practice or business.

Until you accumulate financial or income-producing assets (investments, real estate, etc.), you rely on your human capital to pay your expenses. The lion's share of most people's income funds their lifestyle. We rarely stop to consider how loss of human capital would disrupt our lives and our families' lives overnight. Yet retrenchment, adverse business conditions, civil strife, sickness, disability or death could come at any time.

Until passive income from investments can sustain your family's lifestyle, mitigating the risk of losing your human capital is a top priority. Not everybody wants to work until they die or, like Dean's mother, force others to earn a living on their behalf. Yet that's what will happen if the river flows unrestrained – everything lost, nothing retained. When it comes to financial security, your human capital is your greatest asset. How do we protect and increase our human capital? By means of our financial assets.

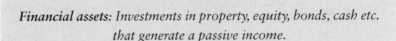

Financial assets: Investments in property, equity, bonds, cash etc. that generate a passive income.

Protecting Your Human Capital

What would happen if you couldn't work tomorrow; if you didn't *wake up* tomorrow? These are sobering thoughts. Whether we like it or not, those days will come. They probably won't come for a long while, but because we don't know when, let us prepare now.

Insure Your Future

Protecting your human capital means providing adequate insurance to do the following:

- Pay for medical expenses in the event of contracting a severe illness.
- Replace your income in the event of temporary or permanent disability.
- Cover funeral costs, debts, wind down your estate and provide for your dependents' lifestyle in the event of your death.

How do you get this insurance? An emergency fund is your starting point. It is a liquid, stable fund equal to three to six months' worth of expenses. This recommendation applies if you're employed full time. If you're self-employed or a business owner, save six to twelve months' worth of expenses.

This emergency fund forms a critical part of your risk strategy. In dire circumstances, our brains lose the ability to make sound decisions. We go into a fight-or-flight mode and are likely to make financial decisions that we regret later. Having this buffer affords us the necessary time and space to think and make rational, calculated financial decisions.

While writing this section, I received a call from a client facing imminent retrenchment. Fortunately, he and his wife had heeded my advice, and their emergency funds were able to fund their lifestyle for six months. In Chapter 3, I teach you how to budget for your emergency fund and other 'buckets'. Together, these savings will help you accumulate wealth.

Alongside your emergency fund are two more must-haves: (1) life insurance, and (2) disability coverage. Buy a life insurance policy that will cover all funeral and burial costs, settle outstanding debts and help your loved ones if you're no longer there to provide for them. Disability coverage will take care of you and your family if you're unable to work.

In South Africa, life insurance providers, like Momentum and Discovery Life, provide cross-policy benefits: If you have a health insurance policy, your health impacts your life insurance premiums. If you wear a smartwatch that monitors your heart rate, have your annual check-ups, exercise often and have positive blood reports, you'll be rewarded. Healthy customers get up to 50 percent of their life insurance premiums back. I recently received half of my premiums from the last five years back, tax-free.

Another coverage option is Professional Provident Society (PPS), a member-owned insurance provider. Like other insurance companies, PPS offers a wide range of risk products. Over time, your membership pays for itself. Because you (the member) own a share of PPS, you receive earnings as the organisation grows.

Insure Your Health

The healthier you are and the longer you live, the better and longer you can provide for your family. Thus, one risk strategy to protect your human capital is simply taking care of yourself. Invest in the health of your body, mind and spirit.

Regardless of our intellect, experience and skills, our human capital is non-existent if our physical bodies fail us. Around the world, skyrocketing rates of obesity, diabetes and other conditions are consequences of an unhealthy diet, lack of exercise, insufficient sleep and high stress levels. When our health crumbles beneath us, we will need that insurance sooner than we had imagined.

To protect our human capital, we need to keep the four pillars of health strong – diet, exercise, sleep and stress management. The secret to lasting success and the accompanying sustainable well-being is a balanced approach. Let's briefly explore each pillar, starting with diet.

The Four Pillars of Good Health
Pillar 1: Diet

We've all heard the phrase 'You are what you eat'. It originates from an 1826 French book on the physiology of taste – and it's very true. The nutrients in our food affect the structure, function and integrity of our skin, muscles, bones, digestive and immune systems and every part of our body. What we consume refuels and rebuilds our bodies, or depletes and tears them down. Although technology has, by and large, improved our world, it has also resulted in processed, convenience food that is high in sugar, oils and trans fats. When you stick to food that fuels your cells, you experience both short- and long-term health benefits, thereby contributing to the value of your human capital.

I learned my approach to diet and exercise from bodybuilding. Inherently, healthy eating is a balance between what you consume and the energy that your body needs. When you're eating more than you are burning, your body stores the excess energy as fat. I find that eating four to six smaller, balanced meals a day works well for me. I can feel and see when I am eating too much and then reduce my intake. Although I generally eat healthy food, I also enjoy cappuccinos, chocolate, carrot cake and the occasional fast-food meal. Sticking to a specific diet requires a certain level of discipline. To me it boils down to the pain-versus-pleasure analogy – I attach more pain to being unhealthy and out of shape than pleasure to indulging in all the tasty temptations available.

Popular diet practices these days include following a ketogenic diet ('keto' for short) as well as intermittent fasting. Each person, however, has to find a sustainable eating plan that works for them and suits their lifestyle.

Regardless of whether we eat keto, practice intermittent fasting, both or neither, we still need to follow the basics of balanced eating:

- Control your portion size and calorie intake.
- Eat regular meals.
- Make at least half of your meal portion fruits and vegetables.
- Consume whole grains only.
- Eat lean protein containing less than 10 percent fat.
- Consume salt (sodium) in moderation.
- Minimise sugar intake.
- Drink enough water (at least eight glasses per day).
- Eat enough fibre (whole grains, low-carb vegetables and fruits).

Pillar 2: Exercise

I really admire the way Fabien, a good friend and client of mine, has synergised his exercise regime, sport and business success. For Fabien, sports, like rugby, soccer, tennis and taekwondo, have created incredible experiences that set him up for life's challenges, which he has overcome through focus. Sports and martial arts have helped Fabien practice perseverance and patience, honing his skills so that he can see clearer and achieve more. By committing to routines that concentrate on his physical health, Fabien never gets discouraged if he has a bad day. He starts afresh the following day – no reason to not be present.

Fabien's investment in his health was his catalyst to achieve more in his career. Every time he warms up for an activity on an exercise bike, he listens to a business podcast or watches a personal finance programme. These lessons inspire him to achieve more in business and in life, and the exercise keeps Fabien strong and healthy so that he can earn more over time, with fewer health problems.

Although being active has been proven to have many health benefits and may contribute to living longer, many people attach pain to physical exercise and avoid exercise altogether. That's why, like Fabien, my fitness approach is a habit or activity that I'm passionate about. Rather than feeling like work, it motivates and energises me for the day. As my wife says, the gym is one of my happy places. This seems strange to many people, as they associate being in the gym with boring and gruelling exercise. Whether it's walking the dog, cycling, playing your favourite sport or doing any other exercise, we all need to move to stay healthy and happy, and to live long enough to enjoy the fruits of our wealth creation. In so doing, we access the optimal value that exercise provides to our human capital, including the following:

- A general sense of happiness and well-being
- Improved mood
- More energy
- Improved brain health, memory and critical thinking
- Decreased depression, anxiety and stress
- Weight loss from burned calories
- Improved muscle and bone health
- Strengthened immune system
- Better, longer sleep
- Relief from chronic pain
- Boosted sex drive

Pillar 3: Sleep

Sleep-deprived people often say, "I'll sleep when I'm dead". Over the years, many health experts and medical professionals have had varying opinions on how much sleep we need for optimum health. Personally, I have learned that without adequate sleep, I am unable to be my best the next day. Modern science and medicine have proven what many always knew – our bodies need adequate sleep! While we sleep, our bodies do the following:

- Heal damaged cells.
- Boost our immune system.

- Recover from the day's activities.
- Recharge our hearts, cardiovascular systems and brains.

Insufficient or disrupted sleep cycles can result in the following:

- Feeling drowsy, irritable and stressed.
- Craving unhealthy food.
- Failing to function at our full ability.
- Increasing the risk of cancer.

Arianna Huffington, co-founder of the *Huffington Post*, is one of the world's most influential women and a modern-day epitome of success. Arianna burned the candle at both ends on her way to the top, and one morning she collapsed due to exhaustion and lack of sleep. Realising she was lucky to escape the ordeal with only a broken jawbone and a cut over her eye, Arianna questioned whether this was what success feels like. As a result, she turned her life around and now advocates that getting enough sleep, exercise and meditation are essential components of lasting success. Arianna aims to get eight hours of sleep per night. Modern medical research confirms that adults need seven to eight hours to maintain good health. That's seven to eight hours every night, not fewer. No exceptions.

Pillar 4: Stress Management

We all experience stress from time to time in our daily lives. Work, divorce, relocating, sickness, a new baby, a new relationship and the death of a loved one can all be stressful. All these are external causes of stress while fear, uncertainty, attitudes, perceptions and unrealistic expectations are causes of internal stress.

Regardless of the cause, we all experience stress at some point in our lives. Stress is a normal part of life and can be used as a motivator to achieve results. However, failure to manage our stress can harm our work and family as well as our health. Half the population says that stress impacts their relationships.[3] More than 70 percent experience physical and emotional symptoms as a result of stress.

---

3 American Psychological Association. (2011). 'The Impact of Stress'. *American Psychological Association*. Available at: https://www.apa.org/news/press/releases/stress/2011/impact.

When we're exposed to a stressful situation, we can lose the ability to function on a rational level. Our bodies release hormones that trigger a fight-or-flight response. Our heartbeat speeds up, we breathe faster, our muscles tense and we sweat.

Our bodies are able to recover from short-term stress. However, prolonged stress results in a lot of wear and tear on our bodies and leads to illness and premature ageing. Physical signs of too much stress include the following:

- Headaches
- Fatigue
- Difficulty sleeping
- Impaired concentration
- Digestive ailments
- Irritability

Long-term health conditions caused by stress include these symptoms:

- Depression
- High blood pressure
- Arrhythmia
- Blocked arteries
- Heart disease
- Ulcers
- Weight gain or loss
- Loss of sex drive
- Asthma
- Autoimmune disease and skin problems

As a child, I have learned two stress management skills from my grandfather. He was a calm, wise and loving man. I recall him telling us two things.

First, when he went to bed at night, he would take his 'worry cap' off his head, place it on his bedside table and put it back on when he woke up the next morning. Visualising leaving his cares next to his bed at night always ensured a peaceful night's sleep.

Second, he placed each problem in his life into a separate box and created rules for the boxes. He would open only one box at a time. When opening a box, he would deal with only the things that he was able to control and not focus on what he was unable to control. Then he would close the box and not continue to worry about its contents while the box was closed. This second skill has been especially beneficial to me. It has taught me to not allow myself to be stressed about matters beyond my control and instead to focus on matters at hand.

Stress management skills like these have proven to be beneficial for many. You can't always control what happens in your life, but with a little practice, you can control the way you react to it and move forward. Managing your stress levels protects you from the negative consequences of stress to your health.

Increasing Your Human Capital Value

Just like turning open a tap to increase water pressure, you can increase the flow of your financial river. Your human capital has value, so it follows that you can affect that value. As long as you're protecting your human capital, why not make it worth more? 'Time is money', as they say. If you're able to increase the value of your human capital, thereby increasing your salary or your profits, why would you not? Even if such an endeavour takes time, it's worth it. Leverage free time during early mornings, lunch breaks, evenings and weekends to increase your human capital. How do you go about giving yourself a raise? Try these tips to leverage your time now and get a big return later, perhaps sooner than you think.

13 Tips to Increase Your Human Capital and Make Yourself More Valuable

1. *Choose to Increase Your Value*

Either we sell our time to an employer who compensates us according to the value we bring to their organisation or we utilise our skills to create a business from which we earn an income. If it's more income we're after, we have to look at the marketplace, decide what the market wants, then increase our value accordingly. Entrepreneur Peter Voogd, author of *6 Months to 6 Figures*, notes that people complain about everything from their salary to their boss, but they do nothing to improve their value. We get paid what we're worth. To earn more, choose to become more valuable. Choose to grow.

Leveraging: Using something to enhance your results, achieve results sooner or make your task easier.

2. Grow Yourself, Grow Your Career

Focus on lifelong growth. Leveraging the value of your human capital differs subtly if you're an entrepreneur or if you're building a career. Like with all success, just wishing for it won't help. To grow your value to your employer, focus on the following:

Be goal-oriented. Decide where you'd like to be in the next six, twelve and sixty months and let your boss know what your goals are. Benchmark income by researching similar positions to your own with other employers.

Acquire new knowledge and skills. Although all learning increases the value of your human capital, it's important to focus on growing your knowledge and skills in areas that are critical to the future of your employer. Artificial intelligence (AI) is now replacing white-collar professions that were once considered safe from threats of automation. Stay ahead of these changes. The future of work is about the heart. We need more emotional intelligence than academic intelligence. AI won't be able to build and nurture relationships. These are the basic needs of mankind. You can future-proof your career by doing the following:

- Signing up for a webinar or online course relevant to your career.
- Reading books on your industry or job.
- Staying abreast of general industry news and events.
- Remaining relevant by understanding the IT tools used in your job.

- Attending conferences.
- Earning degrees and certifications.
- Subscribing to career-related newsletters and blogs.

Many of the skills required to succeed in the corporate world are also critical to succeed in entrepreneurship. Here are some strategies to increase your value to your business and your customers:

- Remaining humble and listening to others.
- Building relationships with customers.
- Doing what you say you're going to do.
- Never resting on your laurels.
- Always innovating.
- Keeping comprehensive records of income and expenses.
- Managing expenses by quitting unproductive activities, releasing underperforming employees and retiring unprofitable products and services.
- Surrounding yourself with exceptional people that you invest in and delegate to.
- Cultivating your team's passions and talents to reap loyalty and productivity.
- Becoming your industry's go-to expert, known for trustworthy opinions.
- Marketing yourself as an expert by writing a book, publishing articles, building a website, launching a blog, giving interviews, running seminars, posting on social media and offering yourself as a speaker at no charge.

3. *Adopt the Right Attitudes*

People hire, promote and buy from positive people. They hire, promote and buy from self-confident people. And they hire, promote and buy from those they deem grateful. To increase your human capital value, be known as a positive, confident, grateful person.

If these attitudes don't feel natural, act as though they do. When you feel down, share an uplifting word with a co-worker. When you're second-guessing yourself, ask 'How would a confident person respond?'. And if you envy someone whose success you don't share, tell yourself that you're grateful for that person. Let yourself be inspired by what they've achieved, and know that like attracts like. Gratitude, not jealousy, will attract abundance into your own life.

4. Become a Leader

Learn leadership skills and display passion, trustworthiness, decisiveness and confidence. The first step to being a leader is to act like one. You already know how to act like a leader. Here's a little motivation that spans over time, through history and in every industry: leaders always get paid more.

5. Network

Networking is making contact with strategic people in and out of your organisation and staying in touch with them. As an employed professional, you're looking for a better, higher-paying job before you need it. As a business owner, you're connecting with future clients, vendors and employees before you need them.

Better to increase your value when you can afford to than when you can't. Better to earn the job offer while you're happily employed than to go looking after your motivation is gone, your performance suffers and you're soon to be fired.

6. Find a Mentor

Up to 80 percent of promotions happen to employees who have a mentoring relationship with a senior employee. Mentors are a great source of information and career guidance. If you can't find one in your company, look elsewhere or find a reputable life and career coach. Similarly, mentorship is beneficial in all aspects of your life, specifically when growing your financial context. When it comes to identifying a mentor, it's important to choose someone who has already reached the level of success to which you aspire. The rewarding thing about being mentored is being able to pay it forward by mentoring others in the future.

7. Be Professional

It's important to assume the mannerisms of success by dressing, behaving and acting the part. Common courtesy is a lost art. You, the polite, professional employee or entrepreneur, will stand out amongst the rude, unkempt crowd. Appearance is everything. If you think of yourself as courteous, don't let people guess whether you are. Make it obvious.

8. Record Your Successes

Most people are taught to be humble, so self-promotion doesn't come naturally. However, if you have achieved major accomplishments or created new programmes, procedures or technology, let people know about it. Especially those people who are responsible for promotions. How can management offer you, the capable employee, a raise if they don't know how capable you are? Whether you work for a company or own one, consider yourself the publicist of 'You Inc'. Update your CV (curriculum vitae) at least once a quarter to reflect your latest accomplishments. Include numbers if possible.

If you own a business, write an article about your or a customer's latest success story. Publish your accomplishments on your blog, share across social media and send to local or industry-specific journalists, bloggers and podcasters.

9. Take Time Off

This tip to increase your human capital may seem counterintuitive. How does taking time away from earning income increase your income? Let me ask you a question: What's your 'retirementality'? Meaning, what do you think about retirement? In our parents' day, people were educated for a career, would stay in that career for forty or so years, then would retire between sixty and sixty-five. There was no point in increasing the value of your human capital. Promotions and pay increases come when they come. Whatever savings you haven't spent by your early sixties is all that you've got to survive your golden years.

This old retirementality is broken, because it breaks us. Traditional retirement damages your human psychology. Remember the six core human needs? When you retire from a lifelong career, you lose your ability to fulfil those needs. You don't have work to look forward to in the morning. No more challenging projects to figure out. Your need for uncertainty will go unmet. As for significance – after a few rounds of golf on Monday, you don't know what to do with yourself from Tuesday through Friday. You feel unimportant to the world. Nobody needs you anymore. Yes, your family loves you, but the organisation that you helped build seems fine without you. You feel disconnected from the last forty years of your life. You may find meaning as a parent, grandparent, spouse and friend, but life offers no obvious growth opportunities. If you're not growing, what are you doing? Dying. As for the need to contribute, if you do something for eight hours a day, five days a week for forty years and then stop, you're no longer contributing to society.

What does this depressing picture of retirement have to do with taking time off? Compare it to the millennial retirementality, the new way of planning for retirement. The funny thing is that millennials don't plan. They don't want to save for retirement, because they don't want to retire. Why put off the good life your entire life until a time when your body is failing? You might be able to afford conquering your bucket list, but poor health won't allow you to enjoy it. Millennials opt for sabbaticals over typical retirement. A sabbatical is a short period of time off from work to do something interesting, learn something new and reinvent yourself. This is possible because millennials generally have short-term savings plans, maybe five- to ten-year time horizons. This time away helps you reconnect with your family, discover new or existing passions, explore new options for earning income and recharge your spirit. Several of my clients who are millennials (or millennials at heart) take such sabbaticals. One client is downsizing, buying a yacht and travelling the world for a year. Another couple has saved up to buy a caravan for a road trip around the country.

Such breaks can be irresponsible if all you do is quit your job, travel for years and return with nothing. You don't want to spend all your money when you're young. If you're taking time off and using some of your capital in the short term, you need to protect your human capital. Make sure that, during your time off, you're increasing your value or reinventing yourself in a new career or business. For example, Microsoft founder and multibillionaire Bill Gates takes four solo sabbatical days a year. He reads fifty books each year, on average, because he realises the value of staying relevant and improving his knowledge – so do you, you're reading this book.

10. *Learn Competent Money Management*

In my financial planning career, I've witnessed several characteristics that are common amongst those with a proven history of earning high amounts of money – and keeping it:

a. Have a plan of action.

It's said that if you fail to plan, you're planning to fail. When it comes to financial freedom, this is right on the money. Financially intelligent people create a comprehensive financial plan of action that they manage and implement daily. In the coming chapters, you'll learn how to build such a plan page by page. Yes, by reading this book, you're increasing your human capital!

b. Set long- and short-term money goals.

Money goals work hand-in-hand with an effective plan of action. Goals provide these people with both short- and long-term objectives that keep them focused and motivated throughout their day.

c. Save 10 percent of your income.

Financially intelligent people save at least 10 percent of earned income and use it for investment purposes or compound their money for long-term gains. More on how to do this in the next chapter.

d. Minimise purchasing liabilities.

Financially intelligent people understand how the burden of liabilities can affect their long-term wealth. Hence, they minimise purchasing liabilities. However, if they must purchase liabilities, then they'll search for the best and lowest price before buying. Often liabilities are purchased from the profit earned from smart investments.

e. Spend money strategically.

Each and every purchase that financially intelligent people make is carefully thought through. Great money managers understand the long-term consequences of making even the smallest purchase decisions. They know that insignificant small purchases add up and result in long-term consequences, such as an inability to pay off high-interest debts.

f. See the future.

The financially intelligent have an uncanny ability to see into the future. How do you acquire such an ability? Use foresight to help identify the possible consequences that can result from each spending decision that you make. Determine if the consequences are justifiable. If long-term profits don't result, then they'll weigh their decision before taking further action.

g. Seek professional financial advice.

Financially intelligent people understand that they don't know it all. Hence, they seek professional advice from experts with a long history of financial success.

h. Interact with successful money managers.

To become a great money manager, you must learn to absorb the characteristics, habits and daily rituals of those who've succeeded before you. For this reason, competent money managers interact and socialise with successful money managers. They understand that through each interaction, they'll gain knowledge that could be critical to their next major financial decision.

i. Keep learning new money strategies.

Financially intelligent people never stop learning about money, finances, investments, property, shares and so on. For them, wealth creation is as natural as breathing. Throughout their day, they listen to an audio programme about wealth, read a book, speak to others about money, attend a financial seminar or read the newspaper's finance section. Money matters are a way of life for the financially successful. Has effective money management become a way of life for you?

On the other side of the coin, there is the majority of people who can be labelled as incompetent money managers. Here are a few tips to prevent the financial self-sabotage that so many people indulge in:

j. Don't constantly purchase liabilities.

Competent money managers avoid purchasing liabilities at all costs. On the other hand, incompetent money managers are pulled towards the temptation of wonderfully packaged and emotionally charged liabilities that lose them a lot of money over time.

k. Don't spend your entire savings.

Incompetent money managers buy what they want when they want it. They're emotional creatures who enjoy the feeling of spending. Hence, they live from one salary to the next. When money comes in, they spend it. When money is not available, they redirect their spending habits onto credit cards.

l. Don't neglect money planning and goal setting.

Incompetent money managers don't put enough importance on saving money, which is why they neglect to set goals and don't create a financial plan of action to pay off debts and move into financial freedom.

m. Don't think you know better than professional financial advisers.

Incompetent money managers don't believe they need help to make wise financial decisions that secure their future. They can't justify paying money to a good financial adviser without first seeing the results in their bank accounts. Unfortunately, the world doesn't work this way. Many such people don't believe in their ability to follow through with the action steps that will be necessary to obtain financial freedom. In such instances, they just don't have enough commitment behind their actions. Therefore, they'll continue to languish in debt until they find the necessary motivation to pull themselves through. Spend money now to earn money long-term. That investment must come in the form of self-education and advice that sets you along the right path.

n. Don't neglect your financial education.

Incompetent money managers don't see the need to obtain a good financial education. This stems from the belief that they don't seem to perceive financial independence as an important enough factor in their lives. Such people also prefer to rely on little hunches to carry them towards financial freedom.

o. Don't follow the crowd.

To an incompetent money manager, any tip is a good tip. It's not unusual for them to gather around with their friends and discuss financial matters, sharing 'tips' and stories. Not only does everyone within this group have a poor financial background, but worse, they follow their friends' advice without question.

11. Adopt the Success Mentality

What is a success mentality? If you want to be successful, here is what I recommend you do. Every morning when you wake up, find five things that you can be grateful for in your life. You may need to train yourself to focus on what you can be grateful for, because without gratitude, you'll never have true wealth. Think of gratitude as a defence against the failure mentality that most people adopt.

Failure mentality leads you to instant gratification. If you're the kind of person who seeks instant gratification, financial freedom is unfortunately not on the cards for you. Instant gratification is a slow killer that will keep you in debt, or just above the poverty line. As billionaire investor Warren Buffett has said, "The stock market is a device for transferring money from the impatient to the patient".[4]

Denial is another manifestation of the failure mentality. Have you ever heard someone say, "I'm not interested in getting rich because money isn't everything"? Without money, how can you be successful? Living in denial is another slow killer that will sabotage your financial success for as long as you let it live in your mind.

---

4   Reese, J. P. (2018). 'Winning in the Market with the Patience of the Wright Brothers and Warren Buffett'. *Forbes.* January 30, 2018. Available at: https://www.forbes.com/sites/investor/2018/01/30/winning-in-the-market-with-the-patience-of-the-wright-brothers-and-warren-buffett/#5450d1e2633b.

If you blame others and make excuses for your behaviour, chances are that you have a failure mentality. To be amongst the 96 percent of people who fail financially, you have to shirk accountability – blame everyone else for your problems and create elaborate excuses.

What do you believe about money? Did you find and uproot limiting beliefs acquired via your financial context? If you haven't, now is the time to do so, before we get into budgeting, saving and investing specifics. Statistics show that most people never obtain financial freedom. Another reason is that the majority have a plethora of self-sabotaging beliefs pertaining to money that keep them in the doldrums of day-to-day survival. If reading this sends you into a panic, flip back to Chapter 1. Nothing is more important than getting your head right. Adopt the right mentality, and new ways to build wealth will become second nature.

12. Act Decisively

Have you ever paid attention to how you decide? What is your process when you make an important life decision, and what information do you consider? Do you process data, or do you just go with your gut? What happens when you must decide as a team or a family or a couple?

Our brain makes countless decisions every day, without us even realising it. For example, in a split second it decides whether we trust someone that we meet for the first time.[5] Daniel Kahneman, a Nobel laureate for his work on human decisions, has honed in on that process. He stresses that human decision-making is flawed and complex. He argues that there are valuable lessons to learn from looking at failure stories and not just success stories. The most important learning is to be aware of the flaws in our decision-making.[6] Common flaws, as identified by the work of scientists like Kahneman, include deciding based on facts from the recent past or the

---

5   Wargo, E. (2006). 'How Many Seconds to a First Impression?'. *Association for Psychological Science*. July 1, 2006. Available at: https://www.psychologicalscience.org/observer/how-many-seconds-to-a-first-impression.

6   McCaffrey, P. (2018). 'Daniel Kahneman: Four Keys to Better Decision Making'. *Enterprising Investor*. CFA Institute. June 8, 2018. Available at: https://blogs.cfainstitute.org/investor/2018/06/08/daniel-kahneman-four-keys-to-better-decision-making/.

universal aversion to making losses. Then there is also the impact of your personality. Some people will not decide until they have all the facts on a spreadsheet. Others are driven by how they feel about the matter. Others trust their gut or intuition.

All these methods have flaws. You can look at the wrong data or come to the wrong conclusions when making your decision. Tomorrow you may feel differently, or the data may disprove your gut feeling. A common error is to manipulate or filter the data until it fits our intuition or feelings. In fact, it's difficult to avoid that mistake because it goes against the wiring of the brain.

How do we make better decisions then? By employing all these energy centres when we're deciding. We make better decisions if we appreciate that in teams and couples, the opinions of others may be informed by their personalities and are therefore valuable to the process. Kahneman says that as individuals we can seldom see the mistakes that we make in our decision-making, but in groups or as couples we have the chance of a better outcome if we value the differences.

Decisions, like moving cities, for example, can seldom be made based on numbers. We must involve all our intelligence centres, including our emotions and intuition. It's not only about surviving on the other side but also about thriving. Become a competent decision-maker and you'll multiply the value of your human capital. An employee who the boss can trust to make intelligent decisions is an employee who is first in line for opportunities, promotions and raises. The same is true for business owners. If the market can trust your decision-making when it comes to how you serve their needs, you'll find yourself with more business than you know what to do with.

13. Nurture Your Mind

We have discovered that our biggest asset is our human capital, being the sum of our abilities. That being so, our minds are the most important part of our human capital. The way we think, what we focus on and how we feel have a major impact on every part of our human capital. We often take the way our minds work for granted, thinking that we feel a specific way due to some external influence or circumstance. Mindfulness is the ability to control the way we think instead of allowing our minds to be controlled by our environment. Mindfulness is the psychological process of purposely bringing our attention to experiences occurring in the present moment without judgement, which we develop through the practice of meditation and other training.

Acknowledging, understanding and developing our mindfulness therefore drastically increases the value of our human capital. You may ask, how does one develop this skill? Here are a few easy ways that you can practice mindfulness in your daily life:

a. Eat mindfully.

When you wolf down your meal on autopilot while distracted by the television, computer or constant conversation, you miss out on the delicious taste and smell of your food. You're also less likely to feel satisfied and nourished because you 'missed out' on the fact that you ate. It can be helpful to remember this phrase: When you eat, eat. When you drink, drink. In other words, don't attempt to do fifty other things when you sit down to a meal, coffee or green juice. Simply focus all your attention on what is in front of you.

b. Walk mindfully.

Take a beautiful tip from spiritual leader Thich Nhat Hanh and "walk as if you are kissing the earth with your feet". In other words, when you are out and about, occasionally pay attention to the movement of your body and your surroundings. Notice as your feet connect with and leave the ground. Feel your muscles moving and supporting you. Observe what is going on around you – the sights, sounds and life unfolding. You may be amazed to find a whole new world that you hadn't even noticed before.

c. Observe your breathing.

As spiritual leader and author Eckhart Tolle once said, a single breath in and out is a meditation. Your breathing occurs naturally and rhythmically. When you pay attention to it, it takes you out of your mind and into your body. You momentarily free yourself from your churning thoughts, worries and fears, and you remind yourself of who you really are – your inner spirit, not your thoughts.

d. Connect with your senses.

Your senses – touch, smell, taste, sound and sight – are your gateway into the present moment. But when you are lost in thought, you don't experience what your senses are picking up. Pause to soak up the beautiful aroma of your coffee; the salty ocean air; the beauty and diversity of flowers in your neighbourhood; the mouth-watering aroma of wood-fired pizza coming from your local Italian restaurant as you pass by. Notice how your clothing feels against your body; the soft, clean bed sheets on your skin in the morning; the comforting warmth of your lover's kiss; the grass under your feet; the sensation of water and suds on your hands as you do the washing up. Put love and attention into the simple tasks of your day, and you will be amazed at how much joy and peace they can bring.

e. Pause between actions.

Pause and listen to the sound of the phone ringing before answering it. Pause and feel the weight of your body in your chair before beginning your work for the day. Pause and feel the door handle of your home before you open it at the end of the day. Putting mini pauses between actions in your day can ground you in your inner being, clear your mind, and provide you with fresh energy for the new task ahead. Think of it as putting energetic bookends at the start and end of each activity.

f. Listen wholeheartedly.

Most of us never truly listen to people when they are speaking to us because we're too busy planning what to say next, judging what they are saying or getting lost in daydreams altogether. Next time you're in a conversation, make it your goal to actively listen to what the other person is saying to you without getting lost in your thoughts. Trust that you will intuitively know the right thing to say next when it's your turn to speak.

g. Get lost in the flow of doing things that you love.

We all have certain activities that we love doing – they connect us with our inner spirit and bring us fully alive. For you it could be cooking, dancing, singing, gardening, writing, painting, hiking, swimming or building furniture. We love doing these things so much that we often lose ourselves in them. That is, we lose our smaller self – our churning thoughts and worries – because we are pouring all our love and attention into the present moment. Incorporate more flow activities into your weekly routine, and your happiness will skyrocket.

h. Meditate daily.

There's no getting around it. Meditation has huge benefits and increases your levels of energy, happiness, inspiration and inner peace. It doesn't have to take long. Even ten minutes a day can have a positive impact on your life. It will also strengthen your mindfulness muscles, so you'll find it much easier to become present throughout the day.

i. Travel or mix up your routine.

There's more than one reason why you feel amazing on holidays. When you're in a new place, you automatically become more present and mindful, simply because there are so many new sights, sounds and smells to soak up. Your senses take over for a short while, and it frees you from your mind. No travel plans? That's fine. Mix up your routine – it will have the same effect. Take a different route, stop at a new coffee shop, visit a new place locally or try something that you haven't done before, like paddle boarding, cooking a new recipe or writing calligraphy. Observe your thoughts and emotions. You are not your thoughts – you are the observer of your thoughts. The fact that you can listen to them shows that they are not you. You are something higher and separate.

Let's review where we are on the journey to Destination Wealth. In this chapter, you learn how to best protect your greatest asset – you. You know how to ensure your family's wellbeing with an emergency fund and insurance policies. You also pick up a few tips to guard your future by caring for your health. And you can afford to do all this as you make yourself more valuable. Let the river flow. Now it's time to strengthen the dam that restricts spending and keeps your earnings where they need to be. Next up, budgeting, saving and investing.

1. Rate the current value of your human capital between one and ten.
2. Compile an action list to improve this value.

_____

_____

_____

_____

_____

_____

_____

_____

_____

_____

_____

_____

_____

_____

FINANCIAL PLANNING SUCCESS SECRET #3:
Accumulate Wealth

Like many people, I had been lazy about preparing for my retirement. Ten years ago, I started working with Dave to assist me to make provision for the years ahead. He has helped me to structure my various investments and to find the ideal balance between property, equities and other vehicles. We set targets and, with Dave's help, I was able to build an appropriate portfolio, leaving me confident that I have provided sufficiently for my retirement. Without Dave's supportive approach and guidance, I would not be where I am today.

– Karl Hofmeyr, MBA, university professor, leadership and organisational behaviour

DO YOU KNOW THE key difference between wealthy individuals and the middle class? I mean beyond obvious differences, like net worth, annual income and home value. I'm referring to their focus. The wealthy prioritise their dams rather than their rivers. Middle-class people do the opposite. They're so focused on making a better living to afford their ideal lifestyle that they don't divert enough income into their dams. Now that you've secured your river's flow today, tomorrow and years from now, let's protect that flow.

If there's nothing to stop your income from slipping through your fingers, it'll do just that. Yes, your human capital is increasing and you're earning more, but if you're spending most of what you make, you can't accumulate wealth. I want you to watch the fruits of your labour accumulate into a bountiful harvest – multigenerational wealth for your family.

Remember, income is your river. Real wealth is your dam. Wealth accumulation strategies focus on the dam, not the river. How do you build wealth as you earn more? I tell all Fisher Dugmore clients to evaluate each financial decision carefully before making it. Will this decision benefit their river or their dam? Only actions that benefit your dam will increase your wealth. Here's why:

Let's say that you're a farmer. Your farm receives water from a nearby river. The water you don't divert to your dam flows to the next farm, into someone else's dam and then eventually into the ocean. What stays in the river flows away. Money that stays in your river is soon gone.

Does this mean that you are supposed to save as much as possible and spend as little as possible?

Many new clients have asked this. While it's important to avoid excessive, frivolous spending, the popular advice that we should simply save more money is wrong. At best, it's incomplete. A savings account is *not* a dam. This is a common misunderstanding. Building wealth and saving money are not the same thing. If your wealth-building strategy is to put money in an account and leave it there, you'll never be wealthy. The money in your savings account is like a stagnant, shrinking pond, *not a strong, awe-inspiring dam.*

Shrinking? How?

Because you're more likely to spend what you've saved on lifestyle upgrades, major lifestyle purchases or survival during retirement. When that money's gone, it's gone. And if you don't spend your savings, then your money sits in a savings account for the next twenty, thirty or forty years and depreciates due to monetary inflation. Unfavourable currency exchange rates can also affect your savings, possibly lowering your future purchasing power – that is, a decrease in how much you can buy with the same amount of money. It just makes sense to allocate your earnings into 'buckets' where it'll grow rather than shrink (more on these buckets soon).

Now, I'm not implying that you shouldn't have savings. If you're already in the habit of stuffing cash under your pillow, that's a good thing. Spending less than you earn is a good habit because you'll have a short learning curve as you learn to budget. Whether you're a saver or a spender, you'll never achieve financial freedom without a realistic budget that you can stick to. Here's what that looks like:

Budgeting 101

If your dam isn't holding back a portion of what you're earning, you can't invest it and watch it multiply. This seems simple enough, but even high-income earners often don't have a budget when they first come to us. The day before I wrote this chapter, I had met with a successful couple who had never budgeted before they became clients. Even though they were both well-off academics, their finances weren't in good shape. They've now realised the importance of controlling cashflow through budgeting.

To put budgeting into practice, self-control is necessary. Life decisions, such as marriage, a new business and signing surety for others, can pressure you to abandon your budget. Resist. Don't be tempted to draw from your dam to pay for your wedding, start that business, sign surety, or for anything else. Your dam is sacred. If you have an impulse control problem that could affect your dam, admit it to yourself. Put measures in place to make you think twice and hold yourself accountable. Refer to Dean's story in Chapter 1.

What if you have self-discipline but resist budgeting for other reasons? In my thirty years of giving financial advice, I've discovered that most people avoid budgeting because they think it's too hard, they think they're already in control or they're afraid of what they might discover about their spending habits. Whatever reason you have for not following a budget, to divert money into investments, we can't delay the right choices any longer. Proper budgeting requires a mindset shift – to the victory mindset.

Military victories, sports championships, successful businesses and every noteworthy event was first accomplished in the winner's mind. They saw in their mind's eye the battlefield, the pitch, the negotiation table. They visualised victory. Then they planned a strategy and executed it with excellence. When you follow these steps with your budget, victory is almost a matter of fact.

Almost. No one knows for sure what the future holds. It's impossible to plan every aspect of our lives. But despite life's uncertainties, we cannot make decisions out of fear. You won't set, plan for or achieve your goals if you're afraid of investment failure. Fearful people would rather take their chances with whatever life throws at them than risk setting wealth accumulation goals and getting them wrong. Winging it offers the least chance of growing your wealth. To give yourself the best chance to accumulate wealth (despite the ups and downs of economies and currencies), you need a budget.

Research shows that having a sound financial strategy and sticking to it is 90 percent of the average individual's financial success. As a Harvard MBA group study revealed, very few people have a strategy. In 1979, Harvard Business School asked students the following question for a study on goals: "Have you set written goals and created a plan for their attainment?". Prior to graduation, researchers found that 84 percent of the class had no goals, 13 percent had written goals but no plans and only three percent had both written goals and plans to achieve them. Ten years later, the students were re-interviewed. The 13 percent who had set goals but not created plans were earning twice as much as the 84 percent who had set no goals at all. The three percent who had written goals and a plan were making ten times as much as the remaining 97 percent of the class. Now, I want to be a three-percenter, how about you?

What's the key to being like the three percent of that Harvard MBA sample group? Focus. Having wealth goals, a budgeting strategy and making daily choices in alignment with that strategy will unleash the magical power of focus. Self-discipline, willpower, motivation and rewards are all important ingredients in achieving success, but the most important ingredient that guarantees success is focus. We all have GPS-like technology in our brains that results in us achieving what we focus on. If building long-term wealth that we can live off is the goal, a proper budget is the roadmap to get there. How do you get started?

Your budget need not be complicated or scary. A budget is simply a plan for how much money from each pay cheque you'll put aside, and where you'll put it. What's important is that you record all income and expenses. I recommend digital or physical spreadsheets to make it easier to refer to your budget going forward. Consistency makes a budget work. Every month you come back to your spreadsheet and look at your income and expenses.

The starting point of every monthly budget is income. That's your salary, dividends, inheritances, alimony payments, rental income and business profit, if any. What if these income streams are sporadic, perhaps twice a month, per contract or once a year? Add these streams together to determine your annual income and divide it by twelve to convert them to monthly income. If you're a freelancer, contract worker or other professional whose income is uncertain, keep your expenses lean. Be willing to live on the edge of discomfort until you build up a twelve-month emergency fund. How do you calculate that amount? Figure out your average annual expenses based on last year's expenses. That's how much you need in your twelve-month emergency fund. During the famine months when work is scarce, your emergency fund can cover the shortfall until your income returns. In the feast months, your excess income can replenish your emergency fund. This depletion-and-replenishment cycle lets you breathe. You know that even if you struggle to find contracts, projects or work for one or two months, you and your family will be alright. Of course, this risk strategy works only if you keep expenses as low as possible. Everybody has good months and bad months. Always live as if you're going into a bad month. Live on the absolute minimum. Take on no debt. Save every rand you can. Thank me later.

Now back to general budgeting steps. After you record your income in your budget, log every single expense. You can't have complete control without a complete record. If you're buying a Starbucks coffee, record it. Don't round up, round down or guess. Record all figures. For most people who attempt to budget, a budget is an estimate. A good budget cannot be estimated. It has to be accurate. Sounds time-consuming, doesn't it? It's pretty easy to record your income, but it's difficult to track your every purchase because there are so many. Don't worry, there's a shortcut. Go to your bank account and download your monthly statement. Have a look at regular deductions, such as debit orders and electronic funds transfers. You also have to look at where your cash goes. That coffee? Smoothies with the kids? Every expense should be inserted in your budget, down to the last cent. R 30.95 doesn't sound like much, but a hundred of those over a year is significant. On a busy day, it's a problem to track cash purchases and to hold onto your receipts. That's where budgeting apps can help. In South Africa, we have smartphone apps, like Wasabi and Mint, that automatically record all purchases, even cash purchases. If you don't like the idea of stuffing receipts in your pockets and remembering to write them down, these apps can save you time and headaches. It's critical to record those cash purchases for one month at least.

Why one month minimum? If you spend R 1 000 on cash purchases, then in month two, you'll know how much cash to withdraw from the bank or ATM for expenses. This works as long as the R 1 000 worth of expenses are acceptable expenses and you're not blowing your whole salary. The most important reason that you budget is to see how much you're earning and how much you're spending so that you can put a control mechanism in place to make sure that you spend the same amount or less every month. If you spend more than you expected to, adjust your budget accordingly. If you get to the point where you're spending more than you earn, adjust those expenses. With overdraft facilities, personal loans and credit cards, it's easy to get into the bad habit of spending more than what you're earning. Before you know it, you're in financial trouble. Regain control by recording cash purchases. Walk around with a little notebook or make notes on your smartphone if you have to. Do it for one month to create a pattern so that you know how much cash to keep aside. Then the rule is, once you spend your cash, you don't have any more.

What's left after you deduct your fixed, variable and cash expenses from your income? Some people have zero excess. If that's you, then it's time to look at what you can cut. Everyone needs to get to a reasonable level of excess in their budget. To determine what level of excess you need, consult with a financial planner. They'll help you identify how much you need to save and invest towards goals, such as an emergency fund, a retirement fund, your children's education, lifestyle objectives and philanthropic endeavours.

If you start with the end in mind and plan properly, you shouldn't have exorbitant debt levels. But if you're starting late, as many people are, and budgeting is more of an intervention than a plan, then you have to include debt repayment in your budget to get out of the negative cycle that you are in – the bad situation. Reduce luxurious expenses in the short term, live on the bare minimum and pay off your debts until your income exceeds your expenses. Your health depends on it. According to a report issued by the Royal College of Psychologists, a person's levels of indebtedness can have a profound impact on their mental health, stress levels and overall wellbeing: "Debt can cause [...] mental health problems. It's tempting to just not think about it – it can be uncomfortable and can make you feel guilty, depressed – or even hopeless" (Royal College of Psychiatrists 2017).[7]

They reviewed the findings of more than fifty research papers and discovered that individuals with higher-risk credit behaviour, such as credit card debt, were more likely to experience depression. Over time, depression and its bedfellows, anxiety and guilt, trigger physical symptoms, including the following:[8]

---

7   Royal College of Psychiatrists. (2017). 'Debt and Mental Health'. *Royal College of Psychiatrists.* July 2017. Available at: https://www.rcpsych.ac.uk/mental-health/problems-disorders/debt-and-mental-health.

8   Villines, Z. (2018). 'How Does Depression Affect the Body?'. *Medical News Today.* July 9, 2018. Available at: https://www.medicalnewstoday.com/articles/322395.

- Insomnia
- Headaches
- Fatigue
- Inflammation
- Chronic pain
- Heart disease
- Weight loss
- Nausea
- Diarrhoea
- Constipation
- Low libido

All signs are clear: Get out of debt by any means necessary. If you don't have enough disposable income (or no disposable income at all) to meet your life goals while paying off debt, go back to your expenses in the spreadsheet. Which variable expenses can you skip next month? Perhaps you can start with no coffee runs. Or instead of five cups a week at Starbucks, have one. You could cut down on dining and entertainment. And what about fixed expenses? For example, look at the cost of insurance and medical care. What lower-cost alternatives are available? Could you cancel or downgrade your satellite package, club memberships or cell phone expenses? If you do food shopping daily or when you're hungry, you tend to spend a lot more. People who budget well, shop well. When I see clients go through tough financial times, I advise them to stop shopping daily or weekly and instead plan their menus and shop monthly as well as online to avoid in-store temptations. When you have meals planned, you're going to the shop with a strict agenda of what to buy. You're not buying a fast, easy, expensive microwave meal. You're buying healthy, lower-cost nutritious ingredients to prepare healthy, satisfying meals. People save up to 40 percent on a food budget just by having that menu plan. Every expense that you decrease establishes your control over your future. As you can see, budgeting is not just planning your finances, it's planning your life.

Unfortunately, most people shave money off their budget when they're forced to because they get retrenched or other life circumstances change suddenly. Out of necessity, they're forced to budget. Don't wait. Prepare now. If, as you're reading this, you're in a budget-smashing crisis, consult with a financial planner. They can help you to plan wisely and reduce expenses. What if that's not enough? If there's a shortfall in your budget and you're going further and further into debt every month just to stay afloat, you may need a debt counsellor or an insolvency practitioner. These professionals bring the drastic financial first aid and even surgery to intervene, save you and reset your spending habits.

If you've fallen into the credit trap, there *is* a way out. Credit cards allow you to spend what you don't have. Many people don't understand how credit cards work. When you have a credit card with a credit limit, you don't pay interest on the first month. You have this perception that you have free money. Most people pay only the minimum amount reflected on the statement. But if you don't pay the full statement amount by your payment due date, you have to pay exorbitant interest that compounds daily – meaning it grows day upon day. Later in this book, you'll learn how to be on the winning side of compound interest. For now, let's get you (or keep you) well away from the losing side.

If you pay only the minimum payment on your credit card, it will take you months, if not years, to pay off. I tell all my clients to use a credit card only if they have total budget control (e.g. your budget gives you R 1 000 a month for groceries, entertainment and so on, and you spend no more than that). If you do pay off the full balance every month, you can *make* money instead of lose it. How? Most credit cards offer 'cash back' on some or all purchases made on the credit card. Settle your full credit card payment every month, and your use of that credit card becomes a small but not insignificant income stream. Every bit counts.

If you're not certain that you have the discipline to use a credit card that way, cut credit cards out of your finances. Use cash whenever possible. It's easier to swipe a credit card than it is to take physical cash out of your wallet and pay for something. You think twice when you use your physical cash because it's a tangible experience. You're aware that you're losing money as you spend it. It's impossible to overspend when using cash because you can't spend more cash than you have in your wallet or purse. With a credit card, it's easy to spend money that you don't have. You think, *Well, I'm only spending this fifty today, which I'd allocated for food.* But you forget that you spent seventy-five at Starbucks yesterday because you swiped your card both times. You didn't physically open your wallet and watch as your cash supply dwindled. In the old days, our grandparents used the envelope system. They took physical cash and put it in envelopes marked, for example, for groceries, entertainment, clothing, rent and so on. Whatever cash that you had budgeted for groceries and had placed in the relevant envelope, you took to the store with you and that's all you spent. Credit cards changed everything. A swipe here and a swipe there, and you're kicking yourself at the end of the month.

I advise everyone who has a tendency to overspend to use cash whenever possible (if they're not using a rewards credit card). This tactic is part of a greater money-savvy strategy. Go on a weeklong 'spending detox' once in a while, spending no money beyond what is essential. Purchase items when they're on sale. Comparison shop. Don't buy from the first merchant that is selling the product you want. Take advantage of special offers, loyalty schemes and discount vouchers. Note that special promotions can work against you. If you bring a R 100 note to the shop to buy groceries and loyalty points bring your total bill down by 30 percent, you can wind up spending a lot more because you're saving money. But then you're not saving anymore. To be a money-savvy consumer, you need to use all the special offers you can but use them with self-discipline. It's the same as with a credit card.

Money-savvy people also know when *not* to pay off debt. That's right, when *not* to pay off debt. Let's say you're paying off a home loan or a business loan. Perhaps you want to pay off your loan early because you'll pay less interest. How can this possibly be a bad idea? Because of that all-important question: Does this benefit your river or your dam? In most cases, early loan repayment benefits the river, as the money saved from interest payments goes to your lifestyle expenses. If the money that you saved doesn't flow to your dam, you don't create any wealth. You use up a lot of capital paying back the loan, which you'll no longer have. In business, we call this 'opportunity cost'. You've lost potential gains from investing that money because you gave it up in a single lump-sum loan repayment.

Good money sense is a prerequisite of financial wellbeing. That's why we want to become smart consumers right away. Ideally, we're planning for sustainable living before life's storms come, so that we can weather them with the absolute minimal level of financial discomfort. Meanwhile, you're also able to afford what your heart desires. For example, to contribute to your emergency fund and pay for your children's education, you need a certain amount of money. That money should be deducted from your income first before you spend on your lifestyle. Without a planned budget to help you achieve your objectives, those objectives are only a wish list. Any well-structured budget has the end in mind.

The earlier you start budgeting, the more you can invest over your lifetime. According to the late, great billionaire businessman and philanthropist Allan Gray, the average twenty-five-year-old needs to save 17 percent of their salary to replace 75 percent of their income at age sixty-five. Let's have a look at Allan's complete table:

Required Savings Rates Needed to Replace 75 Percent of Income at Age Sixty-Five	
Age	Percentage of Salary to Be Saved
25	17%
30	22%
35	30%
40	42%
45	59%

Even if you're in your late forties or early fifties as you read this, it's not too late to build wealth. It's never too late to strengthen your dam. That starts with a trusted budget. Once you create your budget, be sure to revisit and revise it regularly. This will ensure that you're committing enough money to wealth creation and risk mitigation before you spend money on your lifestyle.

There are varying opinions as to how much you should put into your dam every month. Research shows that a minimum of 10 to 15 percent is non-negotiable. Marriott's Simon Pearce advises nothing less than 30 percent every month. If you can't start at the ideal level, don't lose heart. Start small, focus on what you can do and before you know it, your results will astound you. Allocating funds to your dam (even if you start with only 10 percent of your salary) is the most important financial decision you will ever make.

Your Budget Buckets

Now there's money in your dam, with more coming in each month. You've also started mapping out your budget. Good job. Now, you might wonder what that income- and expense-tracking spreadsheet has to do with accumulating wealth. A budget is a mechanism to allocate money – to track your income and expenses, yes, but also to pay off high-interest debt, build up a strong emergency fund and put money into rewarding investment vehicles.

Ninety percent of the average person's net worth results from their wealth creation strategy, and their ability to stick to it. Don't leave wealth accumulation to the occasional whim to put a few thousand in the stock market. Wealth creation is a repeatable system, not a part-time hobby. That's why we're going to add 'bucket' columns to your spreadsheet. Let's discuss effective strategies for your dam that create meaningful and significant wealth.

As you accumulate money in your dam, it's time to put that money in different buckets. These buckets are different investment accounts that vary depending on your goals for them. I advise all clients to commit a sizable yet sustainable amount to their dam's buckets from *every* pay cheque.

Bucket #1: Emergency Fund

Remember this one? Your budget should include a bucket for unexpected expenses, such as having to replace a car tyre, paying unforeseen medical costs, attending a wedding or funeral somewhere or keeping your family and business afloat during a global pandemic or other financial crisis.

Because the goal of financial planning is to sustain your lifestyle at all times, the first bucket to fill from your dam should be your emergency fund as you'll want to be able to access it at a moment's notice. We consider an emergency fund to be a short-term investment. Keep your emergency fund in a money market fund or other low-risk investment –

a savings portfolio that provides investors with income and conservative capital growth, with a focus on capital preservation. In Chapter 4, you will learn more about various investment products that are available to you, the risks associated with each and how to choose the one that's right for your various needs.

Bucket #2: Retirement Fund

With immediate sustainability risks taken care of, we can focus on long-term wealth creation. The purpose of retirement planning is to provide a passive income and to reduce your reliance on earned income. It's essential to fill your retirement bucket next, ensuring that you'll be able to sustain your lifestyle during your golden years. Because you won't need access to this money soon, consider your retirement fund to be a long-term investment.

Why fund the retirement bucket next? There are two reasons. Firstly, it's crucial to provide for a time in life when you can no longer earn an income, before you focus on other investment buckets while you're still capable of earning. Secondly, contributions to retirement funds are subsidised by your marginal tax rate for up to 27.5 percent of your income – maximum of R 350 000 annually. You can invest more in your retirement fund if you're older or if you have disposable income that would otherwise end up in a savings account.

Bucket #3: Aspirational Goals Fund

What do you aspire to in life? To provide for your children's education? To go on an annual holiday to a bucket-list destination? To fund supercars, bikes, planes or yachts? To buy a holiday or retirement home? To establish a philanthropy fund so that you can leave a legacy of welfare to others and ensure lasting societal change? Don't fund aspirational goals like these from your monthly income. I recommend that you fund each of your aspirational goals in their own separate long-term investment buckets.

The number of buckets that each person has in their dam varies. Regardless of how many buckets there are, most people don't have adequate cashflow or capital to fill all the buckets simultaneously. That's why it's important to prioritise which (and how many) buckets to fill first, using the previous prioritised list. An ongoing analysis of your situation will tell you how much money you need to put in your retirement budget. If you want to retire with a certain monthly income at age sixty, you need to be contributing the right amount of money every month. If a certified financial planner's professional analysis of your portfolio shows that you're on track from a savings perspective, congratulations! You still need to save towards retirement, but you can add additional disposable income to your aspirational goals bucket.

When it comes to your long-term investment buckets, how do you choose what exactly to invest in? To protect your dam – and your river – from undue tax burdens, you need a comprehensive understanding of your country's tax rules and the investment vehicles that are available to you. For example, when I say long-term investment, you might wonder, *What? How? Where? How much? For how long?* I answer all these questions and more in the next chapter.

1. Write down how much of your income you will need to contribute to achieve a 75 percent replacement ratio.

2. Now, calculate your current level of contribution. What are you going to change to close the gap?

_____

_____

_____

_____

_____

_____

_____

_____

_____

_____

_____

_____

FINANCIAL PLANNING SUCCESS SECRET #4:

Grow Your Wealth

With careful investing and his knowledge of the markets, Dave performed miracles with our money. We could never have achieved it without him. This has been a journey of faith. We never doubted God's grace and care in our lives. We never doubted Dave's ability or his integrity. I stand amazed at how God has blessed us.

– Glenda Morehen, senior mathematics teacher

'IT TAKES MONEY to make money.'

Have you ever heard that expression? The secret to effective wealth creation is simple: Don't leave all your money in your river; divert as much as you can to your dam. Then use time-tested strategies to grow your capital. This is what we call the money you've accumulated through smart budgeting that you can use to invest.

In this chapter, I show you how to make your money work for you through various investments instead of leaving it to waste away in a savings account. To achieve the greatest return on your investments over the course of your lifetime, you'd be wise to play by the rules – the tax rules. What's next is a brief overview of South Africa's tax policies so that you can keep as much money as possible.

How Taxes Impact Investments

Paying your taxes is a given. Paying too much tax is unnecessary and, frankly, foolish. It's vital to understand your tax environment, and it's not as confusing as you might fear. To understand how to keep as much of your money as possible, you're going to learn about 'investment vehicles' and their 'asset classes'.

Each investment bucket in your dam will be stored in an investment vehicle. For example, an emergency fund is a bucket. You could use a normal savings account, a money market account or a unit trust fund to store your emergency fund. I recommend specific types of unit trust funds for emergency funds, being either money market, income or low-equity multi-asset funds.

Investment vehicle: An investment product that complies with certain tax legislation in which the investor's funds are held.

Now, think of asset classes as the seats inside that vehicle. An investment vehicle is where your money lies and asset classes are the different places where it can 'sit'. Asset classes include the money market (cash), the fixed interest market (bonds), equities (stocks), property, commodities (precious metals, oil, etc.) and exotics (such as art).

Asset classes: A group of assets that behave or function in a similar way in terms of income generation, capital growth and risk.

You deposit your cash in a bank account, which is a short-term investment vehicle. In a long-term investment vehicle, such as a retirement fund, you deposit cash and then use that cash to buy equities, property and commodities.

You could store your retirement fund bucket in a number of different investments, such as a retirement annuity, an endowment policy or a share portfolio. Each of these is an investment vehicle, and within each vehicle you choose your asset classes for your wealth to sit in. In each vehicle you could own several asset classes depending on your goals for that vehicle.

How do you decide which investment vehicle to use? That depends on the tax implications. Think of the source of your income (whether it be an employer, business or other assets) as being on one side of an imaginary border. You're on the other side of this border. Before you can receive your income, it has to cross this border, which is manned by the receiver of revenue – the taxman. You don't get your money until the taxman takes his share.

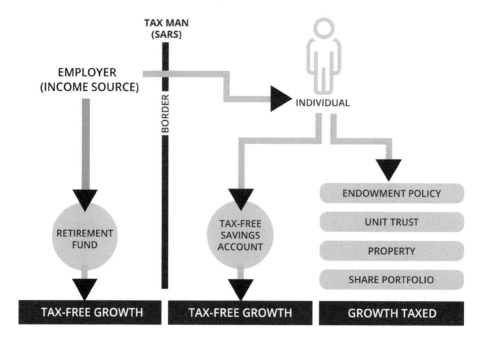

Figure 3. The flow of money from its source to your investments

The following list, although not exhaustive, gives you a short description of the two types of investments available to South Africans. These are 'compulsory investments' made with pre-tax money and 'discretionary investments' made with after-tax money. Then we have a look at asset classes, which are what you buy within your compulsory and discretionary investment vehicles.

Compulsory Investments

When you put money into your retirement fund, you do so *before* your income crosses the taxman's border. If you're paying the maximum marginal tax rate of 45 percent for every rand you earn (on your employer's side of the border), you get only 55 cents of that rand on your side of the border. But every rand you invest in the retirement fund isn't taxed, so you get to invest the entire rand! Furthermore, the growth within your compulsory investments is not taxable as it is within your voluntary investments.

You can store your retirement fund bucket in a retirement annuity, pension fund, provident fund or preservation fund (more on these shortly). You can also bequeath your retirement fund to a beneficiary so that it's not considered a part of your estate when you die.

Research shows that the sustainable amount to withdraw upon your retirement (so as not to run out of money during your lifetime *and* keep your income on par with inflation) is four percent. If you're drawing 17 percent while getting only 10 percent growth, you're going to eat into your capital to the point that your investments will be unable to take care of you for the duration of your retirement.

What do I mean by 'realistic'? Let's say that you're sixty years old and we assume that you're going to reach the age of ninety-four. How much can you withdraw from your capital and still be sustainable? Often my clients say that they want R 144 000 per month from their retirement fund (which has about R 10 000 000 in it). However, the capital would allow for only seven years of monthly withdrawal of that amount. That means your expectations must change. If you're not yet at retirement age, it's not too late to prepare your portfolio so that you can retire with an ideal monthly income.

To retire comfortably, you need a general understanding of the South African laws that affect your investments. The contributions you make to your retirement fund are tax deductible, up to 27.5 percent of your earned income, with a maximum of R 350 000 per year. As your retirement fund grows, that growth continues to be tax-free. That's right, the money that you invest, the interest and dividends that you earn and the capital gains that you make are all tax-free. When you retire, you may withdraw up to one-third of your retirement funds. The first R 500 000 of the lump sums that you withdraw from your retirement funds after retirement age is also tax-free. (This amount is cumulative, meaning that the total withdrawn from all retirement funds is taken into consideration by the taxman when determining the tax payable.) The remainder of your withdrawal is taxed according to the following fixed scales:

R 500 001	R 700 000	18%
R 700 001	R 1 050 000	27%
R 1 050 001 and above		36%

You're only permitted this tax-free withdrawal once in a lifetime. The rules on how easily you can access your retirement fund depend on which investment vehicle you store it in. I'm going to give you the must-know details on each type of investment vehicle available for your retirement fund.

There are three forms of tax on the income you earn from your other (nonretirement fund) or voluntary investments: income tax, capital gains tax and dividend withholding tax.

Maybe you invested in the money market, stocks, property and bonds. Each asset class gives you different growth. A simple bank investment just gives you interest. In South Africa, that interest is fully taxed once you go over the annual tax-free limit. For people under sixty-five, that's R 24 000. Because interest is considered a form of income, you pay income tax.

Let's say that you buy shares of Apple stock. Your investment growth comes in two different forms: Firstly, if you buy Apple shares at $100 per share and five years later sell them at $150 per share, you've made a profit. That growth is called 'capital gain'. On that you pay capital gains tax. Secondly, while you held those shares, as Apple made a profit every year, they gave dividends to their shareholders. This growth is called 'annual dividends', and on that you pay a dividend withholding tax.

Now on to the compulsory investments and how tax laws impact each.

Retirement Annuities

Retirement annuities are often used by self-employed people or those whose employers don't have a pension or provident fund. Pension or provident fund members can also contribute to a retirement annuity, as long as the total contribution to all their retirement funds doesn't exceed 27.5 percent of their income, with a maximum contribution of R 350 000 per year. Retirement age can be any age after fifty-five. Withdrawing from your retirement annuity before age fifty-five is not permitted.

There are two types of retirement annuities: unit trust-linked retirement annuities and underwritten retirement annuities provided by life insurance companies.

Unit trust-linked retirement annuities are more flexible. They're invested with linked investment service providers (LISP). These providers permit you to move your money from one unit trust to another, which allows you to actively manage your investment portfolio. You can also change your contribution amount, make lump-sum contributions or even stop-and-start contributions with no penalties.

You can also transfer your retirement annuity to another listed company. If your chosen LISP doesn't offer the customer service you desire or their fees increase, you might want to switch. As long as you'll receive quality service with a new LISP, I suggest that you switch to enjoy lower fees.

Underwritten retirement annuities will charge penalties in these instances when you move money from one account provider to another. I'm not very positive about underwritten retirement annuities. They're expensive. The life insurance industry worldwide has always had a lot of smoke and mirrors. They promise long-term growth but don't show the cost of getting there. If the insurance provider charges a four percent fee while you're earning an 18 percent return on your money, that's not bad. But in current times, most returns are down to around eight percent; a four percent return is unacceptable because inflation is four percent annually. So, you're not actually earning anything! That's why unit trust-linked retirement annuities are attractive – they disclose their fees, they're transparent and they're cost-effective.

Pension Funds

A pension fund is an investment vehicle that is set up by your employer to help you save for retirement. Usually a percentage of each salary is automatically contributed to your pension fund. Remember, these contributions are also tax deductible.

According to the rules of this particular fund, the earliest retirement age is fifty-five. Legislation discourages us from withdrawing funds before retirement. The government wants retirees to take care of themselves as much as possible. You can withdraw from your pension fund only upon retirement, death, disability or resignation. When you retire, you can withdraw only up to one-third of your capital (the money you originally put in, not including interest earned) from your pension. You then pay tax on the money you withdraw (according to the scales discussed earlier). Investment growth in your pension remains tax-free. Then you must use the remainder of your pension to buy an annuity, of which there are several.

A living annuity allows you to draw annually from your investment, at least 2.5 percent but no more than 17.5 percent of the annual value of the total capital that you have on the policy at the anniversary date.

With a life annuity, you take your two-thirds of capital to an investment or insurance company and say, "Here I am. I'm sixty-five years old. If I give you this lump sum of money, what type of income would you give me for the rest of my life?". This option gives you a high income for the rest of your life, but that income ceases upon your death.

Another life annuity option is a joint life annuity, which carries on paying until the longer-living spouse passes away.

A fourth annuity is called a 'guaranteed annuity', which pays you a guaranteed high income for the lifetime of the annuitant with a minimum of ten years in the event of the annuitant's death.

And still a fifth option is a capital underwritten guarantee. When you pass away, the remaining original capital amount gets reimbursed to your beneficiary.

The best life annuity for you depends entirely on your situation. For example, a widower with no dependents is concerned only about providing himself with the best possible income for the remainder of his lifetime. Such individuals need not be concerned about what happens to the capital (if there's any left) after death. Whereas somebody who is married with children may want to provide for their spouse and dependents after their death.

Lastly, there is the hybrid annuity, which offers higher reward and lower risk. It can give you a guaranteed minimum income over your lifetime that is not affected by market declines. But if the market performs well, your income increases.

In South Africa's Pension Fund Act, Regulation 28 determines what percentage of a pension fund's assets may be invested in various asset classes. And they have certain limitations, such as you're not allowed to invest more than 30 percent of your assets in offshore investments and you're not allowed to invest more than 75 percent in equities and shares. At least 25 percent has to be in prudential assets – cash, bonds and property – within the retirement annuity.

Provident Funds

A provident fund is similar to a pension fund with two notable differences:

- Contributions you make are *not* tax deductible.
- You can withdraw the full amount as soon as you retire.

Legislation on provident funds removing these differences was passed in 2016. However, an impasse between the South African government and the major trade unions has resulted in this legislation not being signed into law. If the new law does take effect, then provident funds, for all practical purposes, will no longer differ from pension funds.

Preservation Funds

Typically, a pension fund or provident fund is provided by your employer. If you leave that employer before retirement (due to resignation or retrenchment), you can't be a member of that fund anymore. But you can *transfer* your pension or provident fund into a preservation fund. Depending on whether you had a pension or a provident fund, you'll transfer it into a pension preservation fund or a provident preservation fund (a mouthful, yes, but fairly self-explanatory). This is what we call a 'transfer between approved funds'. You don't get penalised because it's still a compulsory investment. It's just moving from one compulsory fund to another. As long as the money stays on the employer's side of the tax border, it stays compulsory money, and there's no tax on transfers between funds.

Your capital (the money that you have put in) is transferred tax-free, along with all the interest that you have earned. The full benefits and the rules of the original fund apply to the preservation fund. A single withdrawal from your preservation fund before retirement is sometimes permitted, but it is taxed according to the ruling tax legislation at the time of your withdrawal.

Once you transfer your capital to the preservation fund, you can no longer add money to it (i.e., no monthly or ad hoc contributions). You can actively manage your preservation fund, and if it's invested with a LISP, most unit trusts can be selected. A preservation fund provided by a LISP allows you to structure your own unit trust within it. The law states that at least 25 percent of your preservation fund must be invested in prudential assets.

Discretionary Investments

Discretionary investments (also known as 'voluntary') are funded with money that you've already paid taxes on, such as your income from a job or business. Still, you will be taxed on both the interest earned and the capital gained from overall growth if or when you sell (e.g., if you sell a property at a higher price than you purchased it for). Discretionary investments include unit trust funds, exchange-traded funds, endowment policies, property investments, share portfolios, offshore investments and tax-free savings accounts.

Unit Trust Funds

A unit trust is a collective fund owned by many investors and managed by a professional investment manager. A unit trust can contain cash, bonds, property, equity and commodities. As an investor, you buy units in the trust. A unit entitles you to proportional ownership of the assets in the trust, so you get a portion of any income that the assets earn. Unit trusts allow you to diversify your portfolio between different asset classes and different investments. You can invest in unit trusts with your retirement money and with your after-tax income.

A unit trust must be registered with the Financial Sector Conduct Authority (FSCA), and its assets are regulated and classified by category. Unit trusts are also self-regulated by the Association for Savings and Investment South Africa (ASISA). ASISA sets additional rules and guidelines for unit trust suppliers to ensure quality and sustainability. Every unit trust is owned by a ManCo, or managing company. The ManCo takes ultimate responsibility for the investments, administration and compliance and oversees the management of the fund. A board of trustees is appointed for every unit trust fund to ensure that the ManCo does its job.

A unit trust is one of the safest investment vehicles to use. You can choose to manage your unit trust actively or passively. What's the difference? Active investing is what the likes of Warren Buffett does. He (or his fund managers) are doing ongoing research on the companies, bonds, properties and so on, that are available for him to invest in. If you want your unit trust actively managed, you might hire a fund manager who does the due diligence for you, for which you will be charged a fee.

Active investment strategy: Where the portfolio manager makes specific investments with the purpose of outperforming an index or target return.

With passive management, you're not paying somebody to manage your investments; you're simply sitting back and allowing your money to grow. Instead of buying Amazon, Porsche or ExxonMobil shares, you might buy an index fund, which is a collection of stock in multiple companies, often hundreds. This gives you exposure to a lot of top companies in certain fields and minimises the risk to your unit trust if one company should fail. Ironically, most active fund managers never beat passive management. Which begs the question: Why are they there? I've often heard of investors experiencing a massive loss within their portfolio under the watch of a fund manager, and they have to replace that manager with another in the hopes of earning back the losses. For most investors, it's safer to pair passive unit trust management with a stable index fund than to take risks on individual company stocks.

Passive investment strategy: An investment strategy that tracks an index or portfolio and does not require active management.

Whether you choose active or passive management, if you decide to put money in a unit trust, be sure to familiarise yourself with the terms and conditions of that particular fund. It's important to know its accessibility (which varies depending on the trust), investment horizon, risk profile and benchmark. Some unit trusts invest in single asset classes (i.e., equities or bonds) while others invest in a range of different asset classes. The ManCo decides when to increase or decrease exposure to a specific asset based on where the highest value is. Unit trusts' asset values adjust at the end of each trading day.

There are a number of ways in which you could set up a unit trust. You could research different unit trust companies in South Africa. Many have online portals where you can create a profile and start investing without using a financial adviser. In fact, you can access almost all investments without using an adviser. But there's a lot more to selecting a unit trust than going online, finding one and saying to yourself, "Wow, this one performed so well last year, let me invest in it!". Before you dive into this investment, let me ask you: Is your emergency fund fully funded yet? Remember, a balanced financial plan requires doing the right thing at the right time. Fill the priority buckets first before you put money where there's risk, even a small amount of risk. Why this word of caution? Because even the safest unit trust with index funds can give a 13 percent return in the first year and a 14 percent loss the next year. Only the uninformed put all their money in one place.

Buying any investment vehicle without speaking with an adviser first would be like going online and buying cholesterol medication after taking your blood pressure at home. You should probably see a doctor first!

Exchange-traded Funds

Exchange-traded funds (ETFs) are investment vehicles that are listed and traded on a stock exchange. This means that ETFs' asset values change during a trading day. ETFs track the performance of a group of assets made up of shares, bonds, commodities or property. ETFs are a bit like index funds. An ETF also has units that you buy, but unlike unit trusts, ETFs are listed on the stock exchange. ETFs consist only of indexes, which are passive funds. (You don't get an actively managed ETF.) It's either the gold index, the S&P 500, a shared index or an economic index. From an investment point of view, there's no difference between an ETF and a unit trust. It's just a different way of doing the same thing. One is listed on the stock exchange, and the other one is unitised by a ManCo.

There's a perception that ETFs are cheaper than unit trusts, but that's not necessarily true. There's a perception that Apple is the best computer in the world, but Dell makes a damn good computer.

ETFs can be bought or sold quickly and are cost-effective. ETFs are regulated by both the Johannesburg Stock Exchange (JSE) and the Financial Sector Conduct Authority (FSCA), so you're protected from unjust treatment.

Endowment Policy

An endowment policy is an investment vehicle that holds an underlying investment fund. The underlying investment fund would typically be a unit trust or a life insurance company's asset management fund.

Endowment policies are used by people whose marginal tax rate exceeds 30 percent. The endowment policy's tax is withheld at a rate of 30 percent, saving you taxes on the money that you invest in it. The money that you make in endowment policies is therefore not taxable. An endowment's minimum investment term is five years. Limited access to the money is allowed in the first five years.

Endowment policies can be left to a beneficiary and can therefore be paid directly to them relatively quickly, without being tied up in the deceased person's estate. Endowment policies can also be ceded as security for a loan, and joint ownership is also possible.

Property Investment

Property investing involves the purchasing, ownership, management, rental and sale of real estate for profit. Property is a long-term investment with limited liquidity relative to other investments. The benefit of property investment is that you can leverage the property through a mortgage bond, obtaining a bigger, more expensive asset. You pay for the mortgage bond with your rental income on the property. However, property is capital-intensive and cashflow-dependent. Property investments offer capital stability as well as income and capital growth. Because property is an asset class in itself, we cover it in more depth later.

In South Africa, this type of investment can produce remarkable outcomes. Property investments have helped Fisher Dugmore Group client Nhlamulo Ngobeni break free from debt. After he graduated with a master's degree in architecture, Nhlamulo got a job at a large firm but struggled to live on his R 8 000 salary. He had to look elsewhere for income, and rental property was the solution. After reading a statistic that one percent of South Africans own more than six properties, Nhlamulo decided that he would join the one percent. This buying-and-renting strategy not only enabled Nhlamulo to pay his bills and save up extra cash but also allowed him to pay off his master's degree student loan with his property investment income. While property investing is not a get-rich-quick scheme, for thoughtful and diligent investors like Nhlamulo, it can be a get-financially-free-sooner strategy.

Share Portfolio

A share portfolio is a portfolio of assets you own directly, such as equities and bonds. Share portfolios can be managed by you or by your stockbroker. They can be complex and risky and therefore require expert knowledge or advice. A share portfolio is a long-term investment. Such investors pick and choose which companies they want in their portfolio, usually fewer than five hundred, which implies a higher level of risk than an index unit trust or ETF.

Share portfolios have a barrier to entry. Typically, you need a minimum of R 3 000 000 to buy an individualised share portfolio. That said, if you bought an S&P 500 index unit trust or ETF, you could own shares in the top five hundred companies for just R 1 000. This is how the average person accesses a portfolio of companies. Wealthy people gather around at braais talking about their share portfolios in the same way that ordinary people talk about their favourite sports teams. To enter certain social groups, you have to have your own yacht, private jet, Clifton holiday home and share portfolio.

Offshore Investments

South African investors may physically transfer funds to a foreign currency and invest in international investment vehicles. These vehicles are by and large the same as the voluntary/discretionary vehicles discussed above.

South Africans are allowed to invest R 10 000 000 per year in offshore investments, an amount appropriately called the 'foreign investment allowance'. To begin the offshore investment process, you must receive clearance from the South African Revenue Service (SARS) and the South African Reserve Bank. Once you do that, you can transfer funds to a bank account where currency conversion will take place (e.g., rands to dollars). Then you may transfer funds to an offshore investment or to another bank account for investment at a later date.

Tax-Free Savings Account

The South African government introduced tax-free savings accounts (TFSAs) in 2015. Each person may deposit R 36 000 per year or R 3 000 per month (subject to annual revision), with lifetime maximum contributions of R 500 000. Contributions that are made to a TFSA are after tax, but your growth on the funds are all tax-free. The fact that the returns are tax-free will result in a significantly higher return than a taxable discretionary investment. The TFSA is the only discretionary investment that offers tax-free growth. You can get your tax-free savings account online or through your financial adviser.

In your TFSA, you could have cash, bonds, properties, commodities or equities, just as in a unit trust, retirement annuity or ETF. If your cash was in a money market, you'd be earning interest. If you owned shares, you could have capital growth and dividends. If you owned a property, you'd earn rental income.

Everyone in South Africa should have a TFSA. Why? Let's compare TFSAs to unit trusts. Let's say you had R 1 000 in a unit trust portfolio, and it has grown to R 2 000. In addition, you earned R 100 in interest and R 100 in dividends from this investment over the investment period. You would pay R 45 tax on the interest, R 20 in dividend withholding tax and R 180 in capital gains tax upon withdrawal. But if you had that same amount of money in a tax-free savings account, you would pay *zero* tax (assuming a maximum marginal tax rate and that the person had utilised their taxable interest and capital gains tax exemptions).

This may seem too good to be true, but for once in life, the old cliché proves untrue. The South African government wants to incentivise the population to invest their money and therefore have a lower dependence on the state throughout retirement. Not that the state can provide very much in the form of benefits, but that's a topic for another book.

The Right Asset Classes

Once you're armed with the knowledge of the tax landscape in South Africa and how it affects various investment vehicles and asset classes, you can prioritise the filling of your investment buckets. Choosing the appropriate investment is a process of considering risk.

Let's say that you want to invest money to go on vacation next year. You put your savings into high-yielding, high-risk equities. That would be a serious risk because investment in equities should typically be seen as a long-term, seven-year-plus investment. The contrary is also true. If you're using a short-term savings vehicle for the long term, you won't get the required growth.

Some people consider themselves risk-averse, preferring to invest nothing at all or simply keeping their savings in a bank account. Not investing is just as big a risk as investing in the wrong asset class at the wrong time.

There are several basic asset classes that you can invest in, either directly (with property investment or share portfolios) or within an investment vehicle. The asset classes are cash, bonds, commodities, equities, property and exotics. You've met a few of these already in this chapter. Let's now look at each asset class in-depth to see where they stand on risk.

Money Market (Cash)

Cash is an asset class that refers to certificates of deposit, bankers' assurances, promissory notes and company commercial paper. Money market assets have a short maturity period, pay interest and are among the lowest-risk investments.

Money market funds are ideal for short-term investments (one to twelve months) and would be perfect for saving for that vacation next year. They offer low fees and allow immediate access to funds. Interest earned from these cash investments is taxable, and returns typically don't outperform inflation in the medium to long term.

Fixed Interest Market (Bonds)

Bonds are loans that you make to governments or large companies that pay you interest over a set period, with an agreement to repay your capital at the end of that period. Bond values go up when interest rates go down and, they go down when interest rates go up.

Bonds are a medium- to long-term investment – three to ten years. They offer higher interest rates than cash/money market investments, but they have a higher risk level due to their fluctuating interest. Your interest earned from bonds is taxable. You will also have to pay capital gains tax on your capital growth. Returns on bonds most often outperform inflation.

Equities (Stocks)

Often referred to as stocks or shares, equities are the interest in or share of a public company listed on the stock exchange. As a shareholder, you receive income from your equities in the form of dividends. The share price is influenced by these earnings and the expectation of future earnings.

Equities should be viewed as a medium- to long-term investment – five to ten years plus. They're more volatile than bonds, yet they have provided excellent long-term returns. You'll pay dividend withholding tax on the dividends that you earn. If you sell your share for more than what you initially invested (i.e., your capital grows), you'll pay capital gains tax.

Property

Property as an asset class, within an investment vehicle, is usually a property unit trust fund or a real estate investment trust (REIT). Within your property funds or REIT, you can purchase commercial properties that give you an income in the form of dividends and capital growth through the growth in share prices. Just like with equities, you would be subject to the respective taxes. Property is also considered a long-term investment (five to ten years) with levels of volatility similar to that of equities.

The second way you can invest in property as an asset class is through the physical purchasing of a property on a buy-to-let basis. A good property investment is predominantly determined by the property's ability to provide a sustainable income while maintaining its value. When I buy a property, I look at the following:

- Property location: Is it in a good neighbourhood, or will it lose its value?
- Build quality: Is it structurally sound and well-maintained?
- Rent value ratio: The monthly rental income I receive must be at least 0.08 (0.8 percent) of the property value. For example, if I pay R 2.9 million for a property, I must receive R 23 200 a month (R 2 900 000 x 0.08 = R 23 200) in rental income to make it a good investment.
- Monthly expenses: Repairs, mortgage bond, property tax, insurance and so on should not exceed 20 percent of my monthly income.

How do you find the right properties to invest in? You have to look, look and look some more. According to Dr. Dolf de Roos, author of *Real Estate Riches*, you need to follow this process:[9]

- Research one hundred properties minimum, preferably seeing them.
- Make offers to purchase ten of them with a 'subject to' finance clause.
- Apply for financing on three of them.
- Proceed to purchase one of them.

Of course, other investors look at one property and buy it immediately. There are many schools of thought, and the best option is probably

---

9   de Roos, D. 'Property Prosperity'. Available at: https://dolfderoos.com.

somewhere between these two. For more on real estate investing, I recommend reading Dr. de Roos's book.

Once you've acquired a rental property, how do you manage it? You must establish a thorough process of finding suitable tenants, including interviews, credit checks, reference checks with previous landlords and both of you signing a comprehensive rental agreement. Alternatively, you can find a reputable rental agent or property manager to do this on your behalf (however, this will increase your monthly expenses).

Commodities (Precious metals, oil, etc.)

Commodities are assets that can be grown, raised, drilled or mined. As an asset class, commodities most often refer to agricultural products, including maize, metals, such as gold, and energy, such as oil. Commodities do not provide an income; they are high-risk investments and are complex assets. Capital appreciation in commodities will trigger capital gains tax.

Exotics

The exotics asset class includes artwork, coins, antiquities, luxury vehicles, collector's items and cryptocurrency. Don't invest here unless you know what you're doing. These are normally underpinned by passion. Stamp collectors have a passion for stamps. They spend hours and hours going over stamps, looking for that one gem that's going to be worth a lot of money. The same with coin collectors and collectors of exotic cars. I know of a financial adviser in South Africa who is travelling to Italy to collect three Ferraris that his client recently purchased. Each Ferrari is worth more than fifty million rand.

Most exotics are the playground of the rich and famous. Some everyday people do make money with exotics, but it's rare. Some even consider cryptocurrencies an exotic, so it makes sense to cover these next. You've probably heard a lot about crypto, like Bitcoin. Is the hype true?

My Views on Cryptocurrency

You don't even need to know what Bitcoin is to understand that cryptocurrencies are pure speculation. They're not a symbol of value.

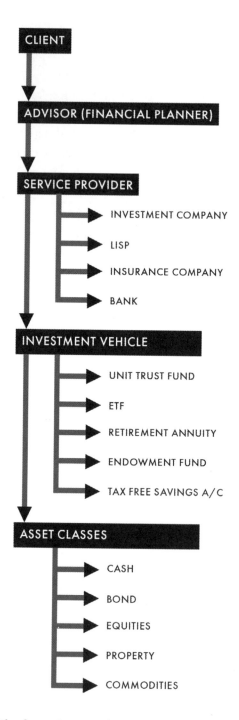

Figure 4. The flow of money from you to your investment.

With the gold standard, currency was backed by a tangible commodity. At least fiat currencies are supported by the full faith and credit of a national government. Even other exotics, like stamps, coins, pins, watches, rings, cars and yachts, have market value.

With cryptocurrency, there is no foundation, no bank that you can walk into, no institution where you can meet the CEO. You're creating an account number on the internet that's showing the value of your investment based on an algorithm that nobody seemingly understands.

Originally, cryptocurrency was designed as a mechanism to facilitate digital payments between parties. It was never intended to be an investment. Along came human greed and enthusiasm at the prospect of getting rich quickly. I strongly recommend that you purchase only legal, regulated, tangible investments and leave crypto entirely out of your investment portfolio.

Sample Investment Strategies

Now that you're armed with a wealth of knowledge on investments, your head might be spinning a little. What should you do with all this information? What should your investment portfolio look like?

You probably know that not every portfolio should be identical. Different people have different personal and professional goals that require entirely unique budgets, savings and asset classes. Only a financial planner can help you find exactly the right strategy for your situation. However, I'd like to get you started in the right direction. Here I use fictitious characters to illustrate three sample strategies for three common life situations:

Sample Investor Strategy #1: The Young Professional

Here's our preferred strategy for a Fisher Dugmore Group client who's just starting out: This person has typically completed their education and recently started their career or business. At age twenty-nine, Sam Smith has recently been offered a job as an account manager. With an after-tax income of R 30 000 per month (pm), Sam's river and dam strategy should look like this:

- River
  - Lifestyle expenses: R 20 000 pm
  - Risk strategy (income protector)
    * Medical aid: R 1 500 pm
    * Disability insurance: R 500 pm
- Dam
  - Emergency fund
    * Objective: R 60 000
    * Contribution: R 2 000 pm
  - Property savings fund
    * Objective: R 100 000
    * Contribution: R 1 000 pm
  - Retirement fund
    * Employer pension fund or retirement annuity: R 4 500 pm

Sample Investor Strategy #2: The Middle-Aged Married Couple

Here's our preferred strategy for an intermediate client, typically a married couple: Don Higgins, age forty-two, and Mary Higgins, age thirty-nine, have two children and own bonded property. Don is a software engineer, and Mary is a financial manager. With an after-tax joint income of R 83 000 pm, Don and Mary's river and dam strategy should be as follows:

- River
  - Lifestyle expenses: R 51 000 pm
  - Risk strategy (income protector)
    * Medical aid: R 1 580 pm (from Don)
    * Life, disability and dread disease insurance: R 927 pm (from Mary)
- Dam
  - Emergency fund
    * Objective: R 200 000
    * Contribution: R 4 000 pm
  - Education fund
    * Contribution: R 1 000 pm x 2 children = R 2 000 pm
  - Retirement fund
    * Employer pension fund or retirement annuity

- Don: R 11 400 pm
- Mary: R 6 750 pm

Sample Investor Strategy #3: The Soon-to-Be Retiree

Here's our preferred strategy for a mature client, someone in their mid-sixties with no child dependents or debt. Imani Nkosi, age sixty-five, is a human resources director and plans to retire soon. He already has a few investment portfolios in the form of rental properties, passive unit trusts and a pension fund. With an after-tax income of R 63 072 pm, Imani's river and dam strategy should be as follows:

- River
  - o Lifestyle expenses: R 51 700 pm
  - o Risk strategy
    - * Medical aid: R 8 500 pm
    - * Dread disease coverage: R 892 pm
- Dam
  - o Investment strategy
    - * Emergency fund: R 500 000
    - * Holiday fund: R 500 000
    - * Supplementary income portfolio
      - Value: R 3 280 000
      - Monthly income: R 10 993
  - o Investment property portfolio
    - * Value: R 2 975 000
    - * Rental income (after expenses): R 13 219
  - o Retirement capital portfolio
    - * Value: R 17 500 000
    - * Monthly pension: R 58 333

Making More with Less

As you might have expected at the beginning of this chapter, it *does* take money to earn money. The river-and-dam analogy implies that liquid assets (i.e., cash) are present before you embark on your great investing adventure.

Now that you've read about everything from property investments to priceless artefacts, you're probably wondering how much money you actually need to start growing your wealth. Less than you might imagine! William D. Danko, co-author of the international bestseller *The Millionaire Next Door*, notes that millionaires reached that coveted status through compound interest opportunities.[10] What is this magical tool that people use to grow rich?

Compound Interest: The Eighth Wonder of the World

The age we live in makes several things in our lives a lot easier through modern technology. Many things in life now happen instantly. As a result, people are lured into an instant gratification mindset. When it comes to investing, instant gratification *does not happen*. Compound growth takes time, much like growing a giant oak tree. Albert Einstein once said, "Compound interest is the eighth wonder of the world. He who understands it, earns it. He who doesn't, pays it".

Compound interest: Compound interest is the process of earning interest on interest over time. It is the result of reinvesting interest.

Let's say that James and Laura are both twenty years old. Each plans to set aside R 1 000 to invest per month. Laura starts investing right away. She invests her R 1 000 per month for ten years until she reaches age thirty and never saves a dime again. James procrastinates for ten years and doesn't actually start investing his R 1 000 per month until he's thirty. However, he keeps on investing R 1 000 per month until he reaches age sixty. Both James's and Laura's investments grow at an average of 10 percent per year over the investment term. Who do you think ends up with more money? You might be surprised. Let's look at their results over time.

---

10 Hoffower, H. (2018). 'The Author of *The Millionaire Next Door* Explains 3 Ways Anyone Can Build More Wealth'. *Business Insider*. November 28, 2018. Available at: https://www.businessinsider.com/the-millionaire-next-door-author-tips-build-more-wealth-2018-11.

Age	Laura	James
30	R 204 845	R 0
40	R 554 524	R 204 845
50	R 1 501 119	R 759 369
60	R 4 063 591	R 2 260 488

Even though James invested R 1 000 per month for thirty years, whereas Laura invested R 1 000 per month for only ten years, Laura's investment value is nearly double that of James's.

The result of compounding is phenomenal, but it requires *time*. Start investing today and never stop.

Investing done right is like watching grass grow. It's boring. The instant gratification mindset, combined with technology and social media, have made the emergence of get-rich-quick schemes popular. The schemes all appeal to the unrealistic desire to gain "something for nothing" as famous self-help author Napoleon Hill wrote in 1935. The internet has enabled these schemes to spread like wildfire, as they prey on this false hope. They have various names and forms, but they all lack the fundamentals that underpin genuine investments. The age-old saying 'if it sounds too good to be true, it probably is' should always be kept in mind (except with those phenomenal tax-free savings accounts!).

The Power of Leverage

Another way to earn more from your investment when you are starting out small is leverage. *Business Dictionary* (2020) defines leverage as "the ability to influence a system or an environment, in a way that multiplies the outcome of one's efforts without a corresponding increase in the consumption of resources".[11]

Leverage is the strategy of using borrowed money to increase return on an investment.

When you use the tax-free investments, mentioned in this chapter, your outcome clearly multiplies.

---

11 *Business Dictionary*. (2020). 'Leverage'. In: *Business Dictionary*. [online] WebFinance Inc. Available at: http://www.businessdictionary.com/definition/leverage.html.

Other People's Money

Leveraging other people's money (OPM) is a well-known and used wealth creation strategy that has been employed by investors across the world for centuries. A prime example of leveraging OPM is with a property investment. Direct property investments enable you to leverage your capital *and* OPM.

Let's say you have R 300 000 available for a long-term discretionary investment. For R 1 000 000, you purchase an investment property, as follows:

Purchase price: R 1 000 000

Deposit: R 300 000

Bond on property: R 700 000

Monthly Property Cashflow		Estimated
Rental income R 9 000.00	Bond repayment	R 6 755.15
	Municipal rates	R 400.00
	Levy	R 1 800.00
Total income R 9 000.00	**Total expenses**	**R 8 955.15**

As a result of using your leverage, you've turned your R 300 000 initial investment into a R 1 000 000 asset. In other words, you're receiving the growth on a far larger asset than your initial investment. I often advise clients to implement property investments as part of their overall wealth creation strategy.

Let's say that Jane has R 130 000 available for a long-term investment.

Traditional investment:

- Investment amount: R 130 000
- Term: ten years
- Investment growth: nine percent
- Investment value in year ten: R 236 736.37

Leveraged property investment:

- Property value: R 500 000
- Deposit: R 130 000
- Bond (loan) value: R 370 000

Monthly Cashflow			
Income		Expenses	
Rental income	R 4 850.00	Bond repayment	R 3 667.00
		Levy and rates	R 1 300.00
		(Assumed)	
Total	R 4 850.00	Total	R 4 967.00

Monthly shortfall: R 117

Another example of leveraging OPM is crowdfunding, which does not require a loan. Rather than borrowing money in an attempt to earn money, you (along with several other people) invest in property or a business opportunity together. Unlike capital-intensive investments, like property, crowdfunders need very little to get started. Organised crowdfunding can pool the financial resources of hundreds, even thousands, of people.

South Africa is the leading crowdfunding market in Africa, with expectations that the industry will reach R 30 billion on the continent in 2025. South Africa has a strong investment society, called a 'stokvel', which was first developed in the early nineteenth century. A stokvel makes a financial phenomenon like crowdfunding more familiar and acceptable. Crowdfunding is perfectly suited to the South African market, where access to capital is a major hurdle. It also doesn't require expertise to research and market a new product or idea.

South African crowdfunding platforms include:

- Uprise.Africa, which has launched several successful companies to date. Most recently in 2019, Uprise.Africa saw R 32.4 million raised for the digital customer onboarding business Intergreatme, the largest raise to date in Africa. Furthermore, a new venture between Uprise.Africa and alternative exchange ZAR X should see big growth in the equity funding space as shares will be tradable on the stock exchange, thus providing additional liquidity to crowdsourced investors.

- Thundafund, which is another platform through which new businesses test and launch their products. The Sugarbird Gin campaign is a poster child of how it should be done. This campaign raised an astounding R 1 086 973 with their introduction to the South African market. With contributions from 155 backers, their campaign proved that, despite that gin drinkers are spoiled for choice, there's still plenty of space in our emerging economy to accommodate new ideas.

  Thundafund also proved their weight in the charitable space, with a project to build toilets for the Mzondi informal settlement. The budding community of over three hundred units faced a major hurdle and health concerns with only four rudimental lavatory facilities for more than four hundred people. With R 68 890 raised in March 2018, a long-term solution was put in place by campaign creators Nyoni Mazibuko and Katlego Mohlabane so that residents no longer have to endure long queues, unnecessary embarrassment and exposure to the elements, and children no longer have to fear injury when using the loo.

- The Fokof crowdfunding campaign, launched by Bellville rockers Fokofpolisiekar also gained quick public interest. The campaign to independently release their first album in eleven years, *Selfmedikasie*, broke records, more than doubling their initial dream goal of R 500 000 in the first week. They raised R 1 081 010 in total.

Other People's Time

Money and time have a few things in common. Managing your time and your money often leaves you wondering, *where did it all go?* We've all heard that 'time is money'. This would imply that time and money are equally valuable.

Research conducted by the Society for Personality and Social Psychology (2016) indicates that "as people age they want to spend time in more meaningful ways than just making money" and "that valuing your time more than the pursuit of money is linked to greater happiness".[12] Regardless of whether we value time or money more, both time and money are important tools to achieve success in our careers, businesses and life.

According to businessman and author Robert Kiyosaki's cashflow quadrant, from a financial perspective people can be divided into the following groups:[13]

- Employees
- Self-employed
- Business owners
- Investors

Statistics show that one percent of the US population possesses 40 percent of the nation's wealth while the bottom 80 percent owns only seven percent.[14] South Africa probably mirrors these numbers. In terms of cashflow, the bulk of the 80 percent falls into the employee quadrant while the bulk of the one percent falls into the business owners and investors quadrants.

Kiyosaki contends that business owners and investors leverage both other people's money and other people's time. Just as each of us has a different context, we all attach a different value to our time and are therefore prepared to sell our time for a different rate to earn an income. Business owners leverage this fact to their benefit by creating a product, process or service that is made of material, work hours of their employees and business processes. Then they sell the end product to customers for a profit. Without this leverage, your results are equal only to your own effort.

12 Society for Personality and Social Psychology. (2016). 'Valuing Your Time More Than Money Is Linked to Happiness'. *ScienceDaily.* January 7, 2016. Available at: https://www.sciencedaily.com/releases/2016/01/160107094105.htm.

13 Kiyosaki. R. (2011). 'Rich Dad Fundamentals: The CASHFLOW Quadrant'. *Rich Dad.* [updated] May 7, 2019. Available at: https://www.richdad.com/cashflow-quadrant.

14 Ingraham, C. (2017). 'The Richest 1 Percent Now Owns More of the Country's Wealth Than at Any Time in the Last 50 Years'. *Washington Post.* December 6, 2017. Available at: https://www.washingtonpost.com/news/wonk/wp/2017/12/06/the-richest-1-percent-now-owns-more-of-the-countrys-wealth-than-at-any-time-in-the-past-50-years.

A Few Parting Words

We cover quite a bit of territory in this chapter, much of which was probably unfamiliar to you. Based on my experience advising clients, it's normal to feel overwhelmed and even a little confused when first learning about tax-friendly investment vehicles, asset classes and compound interest. We cover a few sample investor strategies to help bring clarity, but you may need personalised attention to know which strategy is right for you, before you invest.

If you feel confident implementing the do-it-yourself strategies that I show you here (passive unit trusts, direct property investments, etc.), give it a shot. If you do decide that you need additional support, be sure to find a trustworthy, reputable adviser. Speaking with a professional financial planner is one of the smartest things you can do if you want to build wealth. A Canadian study found that people who have a financial planner for at least four years have 69 percent more assets versus those who don't.[15] This percentage jumps 290 percent higher when individuals continue to receive professional financial advice for fifteen years and longer. If you would like to experience the benefits of bucket-list wishes that are fulfilled sooner, higher income at retirement and overall peace of mind, reach out to a reputable financial planner today.

In the next chapter, we take a look at the end result of a successful financial plan, perhaps the most overlooked aspect of wealth building – leaving a lasting legacy for our next generation.

---

15 Montmarquette, C. and Viennot-Briot, N. (2017). 'The Gamma Factor and the Value of Financial Advice'. [PowerPoint presentation]. Available at: https://www.fanews.co.za/assets/pdfs_2017/15371.pdf.

1. Prepare your own flow-of-money diagram and evaluate whether you are making use of the making-more-with-less principles that you have just learned. Focus on:
   - Tax leverage
   - Utilising compound interest
   - Employing OPM, if possible

_____

_____

_____

_____

_____

_____

_____

_____

_____

_____

_____

_____

_____

FINANCIAL PLANNING SUCCESS SECRET #5:

Distribute Your Wealth

I earned what I own the good old-fashioned way – hard work bound by a strong values system. I learned from my mum to be generous. Because I saw my mum and gran run our household financially and operationally, I believe that women must take control of their own financial independence. I read a beautiful quote somewhere that went along the lines of "The true mark of humanity is not how much we give to those who have in abundance but how much we give to people who have little".

– Shireen Chengadu, MBA, PhD, director, author,
2014 South Africa Businesswoman of the Year finalist

YOU'RE BUDGETING WISELY, paying off your debts and investing money. You've taken steps to grow your wealth deliberately and legally. Compound interest will reward today's decisions tomorrow and in the many tomorrows to come. But what for?

Yes, you'd like to be financially independent in retirement. You want to sustain your lifestyle on your own so that you can bless your children rather than burden them. But more than that, when the time comes, the rest of the wealth that you've grown will transfer to your next generation.

Unfortunately, many people burn through their savings and investments in their old age (or before) and leave nothing but debt to their kids. I wrote this book so that story doesn't have to be yours. Instead, God willing, you will distribute a great fortune to your children's children. And in this chapter, you'll discover the practical steps and the spiritual principles of the fifth and final financial success secret – preparing your estate and leaving a great legacy.

Everything South Africans Need to Know about Estate Planning

What Is Estate Planning?

Estate planning is simply deciding ahead of time what will happen to your assets upon your death. Estate planning answers the question, "If I die tomorrow, what will my estate be worth?".

As with all financial matters, the answer is more complex than it might seem. The possessions, savings and investments that you own today don't automatically pass to your next of kin. Every country in the world has rules about the distribution of one's assets upon death. In South Africa, we have two laws that impact estate planning:

1. The law of *intestate succession* determines how your assets are distributed amongst your next of kin in the event of you passing away without a valid will.
   Many people are under the misconception that their assets default to the government in such a case. This is probably due to the term

'intestate', which has nothing to do with the state or government. It derives from the Latin word *intestatus*, which means 'without a will'.

2. The law of *testate succession* deals with the requirements of a valid will. A minimum requirement that I ask of all my clients is to draft a valid will. That's why we cover yours within this first section on estate planning.

Your Last Will

What are the benefits of having a valid will? You get to avoid family conflict. We all think that our family won't fight over money, but in my thirty years of financial planning, I have witnessed so much strife and conflict that arise from the distribution of a deceased family member's assets. This conflict is always exacerbated when there's no will (or when there's a poorly drafted one).

In addition to deciding who gets your assets, you also get to protect your loved ones' assets. Life partners and other loved ones often suffer financially when people assume their assets will automatically go to their significant other. A will ensures that your assets will be distributed according to your wishes.

You can nominate guardians for your children with a *guardian clause* in your will. This ensures that your children are taken care of according to your wishes, by guardians of your choice – not by court-appointed guardians that you might not approve of.

Once your will is complete, you must nominate an *executor* of your estate. It's quite common to ask an adult child or a spouse to act as the executor. However, I advise most clients to hire a third-party, professional estate executor. Death is a sad and even traumatic event for those left behind. The emotional pain is exacerbated by the fear and uncertainty of what happens next to the loved one's possessions. Appointing an experienced executor takes away a great burden from your loved ones. Because this person will play an important role in distributing your assets, appoint someone honest, capable and efficient. Your financial planner probably knows several such trustworthy individuals. If you do not yet work with a financial planner, you can go online and search 'estate executors near me' to read reviews from real clients and choose an executor recommended by other families. Of course, we all hope and pray that you do not need an executor's services anytime soon. However, wisdom suggests that we prepare for such a scenario. It's for the same reason that we buy life insurance, after all.

By this point, you're probably wondering what nominating an executor has to do with your will. For most people, the first few days after the passing of a loved one are taken up with funeral arrangements and grieving with family. After that, your family members must meet with the executor to initiate the process of winding down your estate. If you didn't appoint an executor, your family will have to find a competent executor themselves to obtain the assets that you had left to them. They cannot simply walk into the bank, for example, and take ownership of your accounts.

During the first meeting between the executor and your family, your executor will gather critical information about your financial situation (any debts that are owed, any insurance policies that are held, etc.). Once the executor has compiled the legally required documentation, they approach the Master's Office in the jurisdiction where you lived and obtain what's called a 'letter of executorship'. Then the executor can lawfully proceed with distributing your estate. During the distribution process, your executor will do the following:

- Open a deceased estate bank account.
- Close your bank accounts and transfer funds to the late estate account.
- Settle all debts owed by you.
- Finalise your tax affairs (i.e., pay any unpaid taxes).
- Prepare a liquidation and distribution account and submit it to the Master's Office.
- Distribute the estate's assets once the Master's Office has approved the liquidation and distribution.

If you plan to have your family hire a professional estate executor with money from your savings, investments, life insurance payout or some other account, you do not have to worry about the distribution steps. Even so, everyone wants to know what happens to them after they die. Many of us, myself included, turn to faith to answer that question. Don't you also want to know what happens to your estate when your time comes?

Guarding Your Assets for the Next Generation

How do you wish to distribute your capital after you've left this world? If I were to draft an estate plan for you, the first thing we would do is an analysis of your current assets. This shows you that, if you die tomorrow, your current estate to the worth of, say, fifty million rand will first get hit with executor's fees. These administrative fees are about 3.5 percent of your total estate. Then you're hit with estate duties (also called 'death taxes') and capital gains tax; the estate also pays for all funeral costs. By now, at least 40 percent of your estate has gone to fees, taxes and expenses, sometimes more. Your family isn't going to inherit fifty million. They may get only thirty-five to forty million! You could easily lose a third of your wealth upon your death if you don't plan for it properly. Estate planning is the process of putting things in place to mitigate loss.

There are practical ways to minimise how much wealth is lost. The simplest form of estate planning is taking out additional life insurance to cover funeral expenses and living expenses for your family. Estate planning can also involve moving assets into intergenerational wealth structures, such as trusts or foundations. These will technically diminish the size of your estate and therefore reduce taxes. Both trusts and foundations are used to transfer assets from one generation to the next as efficiently as possible.

To Trust or Not to Trust

Once a deceased estate has been finalised and the assets distributed, the executor is finished. Therefore, it is no longer possible for the executor to fulfil any responsibilities entrusted to them by the deceased. There is no control or oversight of the affairs of the estate, as each beneficiary will now manage their own inheritances.

If you have beneficiaries who are minors, you may feel the need to exercise control over your assets after they're distributed. Minors need protection and guidance in managing their inheritance. In this case, you would want to establish a trust, either one that takes effect before death (an inter vivos trust) or after death (a testamentary trust). Both types of trusts provide an estate tax-effective vehicle in which to house intergenerational wealth. More on how this works in a moment.

Trusts: Trusts are used to provide legal protection to an individual or group of individual assets. A trust is a fiduciary relationship (based on trust) where one person – a settler or founder – gives the right to another person(s) to hold title or own assets for the benefit of a third party – the beneficiary.

Let's not get too far ahead of ourselves. What, exactly, is a trust? A trust is a legal entity managed by trustees (designated trust managers, most commonly the trust owner's family) on behalf of the beneficiaries (the people for whom the trust is created, usually the trust owner's children). Trusts are generally established for either a set period, such as until the youngest beneficiary has attained a certain age, usually twenty-one or twenty-five years old. This is often the case with a testamentary trust, which is frequently used to house the assets that are inherited by a minor underage beneficiary.

On the other hand, an inter vivos trust is the ideal vehicle for someone who has acquired significant wealth during their lifetime and wants to ensure that it fulfils a specific purpose once they are no longer able to exercise control. That purpose is most often to provide for loved ones but could also be to run a business or fulfil a philanthropic desire, such as helping widows and orphans, disabled individuals and disaster victims or even funding medical researchers to develop a cure for a disease or condition that personally affected the deceased. As an inter vivos trust is established during the person's lifetime, it allows the owner to select trustees who can fulfil the trust's objectives both during and after the owner's lifetime.

Whichever type of trust you establish, you will still gain three primary benefits, which are (1) control of your wealth after death; (2) reduced estate duties, capital gains taxes and executors' fees payable at death; and (3) fulfilment of a purpose or calling beyond your lifespan. For these reasons, it's wise to set up a trust as soon as you are able. That goes for whether you're a single individual or have a spouse and children.

Foundations: How the World's Richest Families Stay That Way

The wealthiest families in the world embed their wealth in foundations to manage the assets from one generation to the next and reduce administrative costs and taxes. Sounds a lot like a trust, doesn't it? The difference between a foundation and a trust is that a trust has a list of beneficiaries. From a legal point of view, the trust is the ownership of the assets. The trust is registered and managed by trustees. It's in the trustees' names. A foundation is managed by trustees, but the ownership rests in the foundation's name, not in the trustees' names.

Foundations are not available in South Africa, but if you have an interest in offshore investing, a foundation could be right for you. Many wealthy South Africans that I know are doing this now. Because there are many legal hoops to jump through for South Africans to set up an international foundation, I recommend speaking with a qualified financial professional about your unique situation to discuss the pros and cons of this intergenerational investment vehicle.

What Else Your Estate Plan Needs

Having your affairs in order can drastically reduce the stress that your loved ones experience following your death. We've all heard that very expression countless times: 'having one's affairs in order'. What does it mean? From a South African perspective, 'affairs' refer to your will, trust or foundation and also to the following:

- Your funeral wishes (e.g., a document or letter briefly explaining these)
- Your identity document or passport
- Marriage certificate (if married)
- Antenuptial contract (if married out of community of property)
- Copy of divorce order and settlement agreement (if divorced)

- Two certified copies of the first page of the identity document or birth certificate of each heir
- Two certified copies of the marriage certificate of each heir (if married)
- Telephone numbers, postal addresses and email addresses of each heir
- Estate particulars of each predeceased spouse (i.e., full name, date of death, place of death, Master of High Court office and estate number)
- Original title and transport deeds, sectional title, timeshare and mineral rights certificates (if available)
- Original motor vehicle registration certificates
- Original licenses for firearms
- Copies of municipal services accounts (i.e., water, light and property levy/tax accounts)
- Original shares and investment certificates (e.g., unit trusts)
- Original policy contracts (if payable to the estate, including funeral policies)
- Details of policies payable to beneficiaries
- Retirement annuities and pension fund documents
- Copy of salary advice
- Copy of short-term insurance contracts
- Copies of hire purchases, lease documents, outstanding accounts, loans or debts
- Full particulars of savings, cheque, transmission and deposit accounts at banks as well as cheque books, credit cards and other cards
- Copies of latest bank statements
- A complete list of all liabilities as well as statements reflecting outstanding amounts (including loans to other people)
- Income tax (reference number, last assessment and office submitted to)
- VAT registration number (where applicable)
- Copies of rental/lease agreements
- Full particulars of medical aid
- Full particulars of pension fund, provident fund or particulars of employer (address and employee number)
- Copy of telephone account
- Copy of TV license
- Information on sold assets during the last two years (e.g., capital assets sold, disposed, alienated or estranged)
- Mortgage bond registration documents

- Business contracts/agreements
- Trade licenses
- Details of surety obligations
- Name, address and telephone numbers of general practitioner (your family's doctor)
- Details of companies, partnerships, trusts, close corporations or sole proprietorship
- Details of bookkeeper/auditor
- My online life after my death (including passwords of social media, email accounts, etc.)
- Full particulars of funeral undertaker (invoice and receipt, if prepaid)
- Original death certificate (in case of an unnatural death, particulars of accident, police office, investigating officer, case number and possible cause of death)
- Information regarding lump-sum benefit (payable to the deceased in the year prior to death)

I advise clients to compile these in what I refer to as a 'death-or-legacy file'. Imagine how loved your family would feel when they discover that you took the time and put in the effort to gather all this information prior to your death to make it easier on them. They will feel your presence beyond your passing, even tangibly so.

A Great Legacy: More Than Money

I have found that the awareness of the need to leave a legacy usually manifests as we age. Initially, most people's awareness begins with the desire to provide financial security for loved ones at their death. But many people's desire to leave a legacy never progresses past providing for loved ones. However, a few people accept the opportunity to make their lives mean more in the long term. Throughout history, many great leaders have built palaces, mosques, pyramids and fortresses that often stood proud and distinct among otherwise desert-like terrain.

Am I saying that you should construct something great to stand as a testament to your existence? No, not necessarily. I am simply acknowledging the fact that we are all born with an innate desire to achieve greatness in some way and, in so doing, to mark our presence in the world. After all, significance, the feeling of being worthy and special, is one of our six core human needs. It's a *need*, not a desire. People cannot live a contented life without it. We all have this need to feel unique and valued. The desire to be special starts at birth, continues throughout life and ends with wanting to be remembered after we die.

Finance guru and content writer Pablo Escarcega recently stated in an article, titled 'The Importance of Being Remembered' (2016), that our egos crave attention and whisper to us that we deserve to be recognised and that, as humans among billions, we do not want to be forgotten.[16] As we all want to be remembered, we ought to ask ourselves what we would like to be remembered for being and doing while we were here.

What Will You Be Remembered For?

Over one hundred years ago, the award-winning American essayist Bessie A. Stanley wrote:

> He has achieved success who has lived well, laughed often and loved much; who has gained the respect of intelligent men and the love of little children; who has filled his niche and accomplished his task; who has left the world better than he found it, whether by an improved poppy, a perfect poem or a rescued soul; who has never lacked appreciation of earth's beauty or failed to express it; who has always looked for the best in others and given the best he had; whose life was an inspiration; whose memory a benediction.[17]

One of the top ten most commonly googled questions is, 'What is the meaning of life?'. To live a meaningful, purpose-driven life matters today as much as at any point in history. Your life is your most precious asset. But because we do not live forever, what will become of the void that you leave behind when you die? Will your legacy live on in your place for the next generation and for those that come after? What will your death say

---

16 Escarcega, P. (2016). 'The Importance of Being Remembered'. *Medium*. April 23, 2016. Available at: https://medium.com/@iamirunman/the-importance-of-being-remembered-822063875877.

17 Stanley, B. A. (1905). 'Success'. Originally published in *Emporia Gazette of Emporia* [BSEK]. Accessed on Quote Investigator. (2012). 'He Has Achieved Success Who Has Lived Well, Laughed Often and Loved Much'. *Quote Investigator*. June 26, 2012. Available at: https://quoteinvestigator.com/2012/06.

about your life? What will your family and friends feel as a result of what you leave behind? Will it say that you were clinging to your possessions as status symbols, hoarding for comfort or holding onto controlling your affairs, even when you were no longer capable of doing so? Will it testify that you lived a chaotic life, leaving messy affairs to sort out, or will it say that you lived a mindful life, leaving little drama behind? You won't have the chance to explain or make excuses.

Everyone desires to be remembered fondly for what they contributed to the world. You and I are no different. Our innate need to leave a legacy stems from our desire for eternal life – we want to put a stamp on the future and change the course of history for future generations through whatever contributions we're able to make here and now.

As long as I can remember, I have always enjoyed the fulfilment that I felt when I was able to give others some sort of advice or strategy that added value to their lives. As I wrote this chapter, I was reminded of three important lessons gleaned from my financial planning career: (1) I've been able to help others put their financial realities into perspective and guide them to strategies and solutions to do the best they could with what they have to ensure their financial sustainability and ultimately success; (2) I've learned that our financial context can limit our potential to achieve meaningful financial success and that so often we are unaware of the limits that we set on our own success; and (3) I've learned that generosity is our ultimate purpose.

With this knowledge, I have been able to make a difference for many clients and their families. Through this book, my business and those whose lives I've been able to influence, I would like to leave my mark on this world. To honour my legacy, it's important that my financial results speak for themselves – to provide financial security for my family and stakeholders in business and potentially keep helping others to become the best financial version of themselves.

You might be wondering what giving has to do with legacy. Many South Africans that I've met consider leaving a legacy and even giving to others as a luxury afforded to the world of the rich and famous. According to Tony Robbins, contribution is a basic human need, just as certainty, significance, love and growth are.

For me as a Christian, giving is a cornerstone of my faith. Malachi 3:9–10 says, "'You are under a curse – your whole nation – because you are robbing me. Bring the whole tithe into the storehouse, that there may be food in my house. Test me in this', says the LORD Almighty, 'and see if I will not throw open the floodgates of heaven and pour out so much blessing that there will not be room enough to store'" (NIV).

According to this and other passages in the Bible, giving is an instruction from God. However, the spirit or attitude that we adopt in our giving is also important. 2 Corinthians 9:7 says, "Each of you should give what you have decided in your heart to give, not reluctantly or under compulsion, for God loves a cheerful giver" (NIV).

Generosity is of vital importance to other faiths as well. In Judaism, the Hebrew scriptures refer to *tzedakah*, literally meaning 'justice'. *Tzedakah* is considered a moral obligation that all Jews must follow. Commitment to justice means Jews believe they should help the poor. Beyond giving just time and money, rabbis even speak of *gemilut chasadim*, literally meaning 'loving kindness' or focusing on a right relationship with others as necessary for religious giving.

For Muslims, giving is one of the five pillars of Islam. *Zakat*, meaning 'to grow in purity', is an annual payment of 2.5 percent of one's assets. But this amount is considered by faithful Muslims to be the *minimum* obligation of their religious giving.

Aside from faith, many books on happiness, life-fulfilment and abundance emphasise the value of giving generously. I've learned from my clients that people who adopt a generous nature and an abundant mindset seem more content and ironically have greater levels of wealth than their peers of a similar context who do not give freely.

Clearly, I believe legacy is more than money. Yes, this book offers sound financial advice to grow your wealth, but death takes us unaccompanied by our possessions. All the material wealth that we've accumulated during life is consolidated and distributed. For this reason, the fifth and final financial success secret includes wealth on an emotional, altruistic and even spiritual level.

Good Money Habits: One of the Greatest Gifts You Can Give Your Children

Proverbs 13:22a says, "A good person leaves an inheritance for their children's children" (NIV). Notice the Biblical King Solomon's choice of words. He could have written "for their children". No, this proverb extends to the following generation. The vast majority of fortunes are squandered by the heirs. Approximately 70 percent of all families deplete their inheritance.[18] By the third generation, that goes up to 90 percent, meaning that most grandkids waste the wealth passed down to them by their grandparents. Let that sink in.

Money is not enough. Without good money habits firmly grounded in a financial context of abundance, generosity and self-discipline, everything you have worked for will one day be lost to the impulse purchases of your descendants. That's why I believe that one of the most precious gifts you can pass down to your children is financial wisdom. There are four primary ways I've taught my kids to manage money well, and I'd love for you to incorporate them into your family too.

1. Talk about money. Having open, straightforward, calm conversations about money is vital. Beginning in toddlerhood, children notice how their parents treat money. Do they take advantage of sound financial opportunities? Or do they hoard money, or worse, waste it? If your kids hear you talking about money in an honest, relaxed way and then watch as you model disciplined decision-making, they will one day adopt those same attitudes and behaviours.

2. Use cash, not cards. You already know why. When children see you spend cash, they witness the value of money first-hand. It's a finite resource. When that five-rand banknote is gone, it's gone. When you pay cash, you'll also teach your kids that you are not able to fulfil their every wish. For example, if you bring your child shopping with you and they ask for a chocolate bar, you are able to quite literally show them the money you have so that they understand the difference between life's necessities and nice-to-have's.

3. Provide an allowance. Pocket money earned from household chores

---

18   Taylor, C. (2015). '70% of Rich Families Lose Their Wealth by the Second Generation'. *Money*. June 17, 2015. Available at: https://money.com/rich-families-lose-wealth.

is an excellent money management training tool. Beginning around age six, your child can earn a weekly allowance. The key is *earn*, not *receive*. Children must understand the value of a rand – they must work for their money. I recommend talking to your kids about how you use your money (food, motor vehicle, utilities, etc.) and offering suggestions on how they can save and spend their allowance. At age nine, a child can have their own bank account. A portion of every allowance should go into that account, with the rest available to them for spending as required. Soon, kids learn the value of long-term savings. They will be able to afford bigger expenses as they grow up, such as a bicycle when they are teenagers. The great lesson here, of course, is that you cannot have something if you cannot afford it. If only every adult in the country had learned this as a kid!

4. Keep teaching. As your kids mature, introduce and explain unfamiliar concepts, such as borrowing and investing, using real-life scenarios. For example, if you take the family to Mauritius on holiday, have a conversation about currency exchange rates when you get to the airport, before you buy Mauritian rupees.

The Legacy Letter: Documenting What Matters

According to *The New York Times*, 81 percent of people want to write a book.[19] Chances are, you're one of them. You feel like you'd be doing a disservice to the world if you failed to document your life, your experiences and your learnings for others to enjoy. And you're probably right.

Am I saying you *should* write a book once you finish reading this one? Not exactly. Having completed the laborious process of outlining, writing, editing, rewriting, re-editing, composing and finally publishing this book, I have good news for you. To author a meaningful work, you do not need to rise at 4:30 a.m. and put pen to paper for two or three hours. If what matters to you is sharing meaningful stories with family and possibly close friends, write a short legacy book. All it needs to be is the length of a letter, so no more than one page, if you like. A legacy book involves reflecting on your life, your values, your family

---

19 Epstein, J. (2002). 'Think You Have a Book in You? Think Again'. *The New York Times*. September 28, 2002. Available at: https://www.nytimes.com/2002/09/28/opinion/think-you-have-a-book-in-you-think-again.html.

traditions, your family name, your family history and your wisdom and love for the generations to come. Despite the fact that so many of us want to become an author, I'm surprised that so few people take the time to write a short legacy book to bless and enrich their descendants.

The written legacy tradition itself is an ancient practice stemming from Biblical times. Genesis 49 tells the story of Jacob blessing his sons. From his deathbed, the patriarch of Israel prayed over his sons and asked them to bury him and his already deceased wife, Rachel, alongside his ancestors Abraham and Sarah. This chapter amounts to a love letter from a father to his sons, passing forward his family's history, faith and values.

Your letter may take only fifteen to thirty minutes to write, but its impact may last for thousands of years, just as Jacob's letter has. One Fisher Dugmore Group client has a family tradition of writing each generation's legacy letters in the same journal – a truly one-of-a-kind family heirloom for generations to come.

To help get you started on your legacy book, I recommend that you write out whatever comes to mind on the following five topics:

Context

Write about your family history, the period in which you live, major events that you've witnessed and basic information about your own life. Imagine your great-great-great-great-granddaughter wondering to herself, *What was life like for my ancestors?*. Then answer her question.

Story

This is your autobiography. Be as brief or as detailed as you like. Does this seem difficult? Here's how I broke through my resistance to writing this section. I realised that it's better to put down *something*, even a couple of paragraphs, than to keep telling myself I'll do it later. Later may never come. Then it will be too late.

Lessons

What gives you meaning? How have you impacted the lives of others? What values do you pray that everyone in your family tree in future will live by? What painful experiences do you hope no one else ever has to endure, to learn from? Record your wisdom in this section.

Blessings

Like Jacob, express your love, appreciation and devotion for and to your family. Imagine that this is your very last opportunity to bless them with your love.

The Constitution

Families who establish intergenerational wealth often draft a family constitution that documents the family vision and mission regarding the management of family affairs in business, in the community, in their faith and in their personal lives. Your constitution can establish a family council to run the family's affairs and lay out your values relating to equality among family members, maintenance of the family business (if applicable) and your policy on philanthropy.

It's not easy to say goodbye. Everything you have learned and plan to (or have already begun to) apply from this book is at stake. If you desire for your wealth to live beyond you and make the world a better place, keep what you read here near and dear to your heart. And while you're at it, get started on that letter! Your legacy can't wait.

A Meaningful Legacy for Life

Sound financial planning, discovering your purpose or *why* in life and extending love and compassion to others are all required to effectively create, grow and maintain wealth to provide for a meaningful legacy.

A clear understanding of who we are and our sense of purpose often ignite a passion to make a lasting difference in life and then to ensure that the difference lasts beyond our lifespans. Most people's need for significance is focused on ensuring that their loved ones are financially provided for after their death as well as imparting their love for those who remain behind and ensuring that their vision and values are passed on to future generations. I hope through this chapter – and through this book as a whole – that I have done exactly that. To the point, this book is part of my own legacy, and I am so grateful to you for sharing your time with me to discover, explore, begin to practice and soon master the five financial planning success secrets. Now the real test begins.

Test? What do I mean by this? From an early age, our parents, teachers and life in general condition us to prepare for some or other test, assignment or exam. And so we busy ourselves preparing to achieve a passing grade at the very least. After our formal education, this process is repeated in our careers, professions and businesses. Ironically, many go through life unaware of the importance of passing 'Life 101'.

Life 101 is taking everything that we have learned and using that to be self-sustainable or in perfect alignment, as referred to throughout in this book. It's ensuring that the daily lifestyle we enjoy is protected from unforeseen risks with a risk strategy, that you are not spending all your money in the river and that you are allocating enough to your dam to provide for an emergency fund as well as adequate wealth creation to achieve your life goals and ultimately enjoy a carefree retirement. That is Life 101, and you are about to take the test.

1. If you died tomorrow, what would you want to be remembered for?
2. What would you want to say to your loved ones if you weren't here to tell them yourself?
3. Use the answers to the above as a basis to construct your legacy letter.

_____

_____

_____

_____

_____

_____

_____

_____

_____

_____

_____

_____

The Greatest Wealth Secret of All

Dave Fisher has been of enormous help to me with managing my personal finances during the many years of my being totally committed to my professional work. It is always good to know that professionals are taking care of what you produce and are giving you security for the long run. The team has done an outstanding job with great personal service, good financial acumen and a clear and structured plan.

– Nick Binedell, MBA, PhD, Gordon Institute of Business Science founding director

FAD DIETS DON'T WORK. They promise quick results ('Six days to six-pack abs'), immediate gratification ('Lose weight eating cake') and short-term progress ('Thirty days to a healthier you'). Even though I'm not a weight-loss expert, I say this with confidence because studies show that dieting ultimately *worsens* a dieter's health.[20] Yes, if you desire to lose and keep off unwanted weight, one of the worst things you can do is go on a diet.

It's been my experience that most people treat their finances like a diet. Anyone can say that they want to eat healthier; likewise, anyone can say that they want to save more and spend less. That's easy. But without a sustainable strategy for the long term, you cannot create a new habit in either case. Diets fail to fulfil their promises because they don't result in permanent change. If you were to treat investing like giving up sugar for a month, what would happen when your motivation fades? You'd fill your shopping basket with sweets, and you'd divert your river into a Mediterranean cruise. No emergency fund yet? No budget? Massive credit card debt? Then it's not time to go on holiday.

Financially successful people stick with a strategy that works – they follow the five secrets in this book, even when they don't feel like it, because they know the alternative. Letting yourself get lax with your spending habits puts you at risk of losing everything that you've worked for. I have a friend who recently purchased a home that was priced well above his means. When he was retrenched soon after, he and his family plunged into a pool of stress. With no emergency fund, they had to downsize and sell their possessions, including the new house.

That's why I want to remind you of the importance of the long term. You're forming new habits around earning, spending and investing. For most people, these habits feel unnatural at first. This is the way of every new habit. Imagine moving to a society with entirely different cultural customs. You would be completely out of your comfort zone, but things would be normal for those around you. Over time, this new society would begin to feel normal to you as well. So it is with new ways to think about money.

---

20   University of California – Los Angeles. (2007). 'Dieting Does Not Work, Researchers Report'. *ScienceDaily*. April 5, 2007. Available at: https://www.sciencedaily.com/releases/2007/04/070404162428.htm.

It's natural to experience a phase of discomfort as you budget – perhaps for the first time – and watch as your take-home pay dwindles because you are leveraging pre-tax investment opportunities. Let any uncomfortable feelings serve as a reminder that you're upgrading your financial context. Before reading this book, you probably didn't know how you had been programmed to think about money. Now you have the opportunity to change.

You may get side-tracked and be tempted to revert back to the way you've always spent money. Resist. Financial success is more about the journey than the destination. After all, the final destination is death, and you won't be taking your wealth with you. That's why it matters that we take care of ourselves and our families while we can, providing for them and the causes we care about after we're gone.

Apply what you've learned in this book, and I assure you that your financial context will change. New habits will replace old ones. You'll finally savour financial sustainability and success. Regardless of your lifestyle desires or any financial disasters that you may experience, stick with the plan. And remember, there's never a wrong time to reach out for professional financial support.

That's exactly what Fisher Dugmore clients Wally and Glenda did twenty years before the time of this writing. In January 2000, Wally's boss was tragically killed in a car crash. Within a week, his family closed the company, leaving all the staff jobless. At the time, Wally and Glenda had no medical aid, almost no pension and an income tax mess. The late owner had been deducting all of those from Wally's salary but had not paid it into the relevant funds. Both their daughters were in university, with the elder planning a June wedding. All they had to live on was Glenda's governing body post, teaching mathematics.

A few weeks into their financial trials, they shared with their church congregation what had happened. Suddenly, everyone rushed to their aid, giving them money, food and helping with the wedding. One of the members who they had asked to help was me. "We can put a financial plan together to take you where you need to be," I told Wally and Glenda.

Immediately, they started contributing R 400 per month into a low-risk investment product, a retirement annuity. As soon as Wally secured employment, they increased this. The couple's first goal was to reach R 1 000 000 by Wally's retirement in 2015. Several years prior, they hit that number and said why not go for R 2 000 000? When Wally retired in April 2017, their savings amounted to R 4 000 000. Then, when Glenda retired in 2020, their portfolio value was in excess of R 5 000 000, even though they had drawn down for more than two years and paid for their daughter's medical school tuition and the other's accounting education.

What amazes me most about their story is the fact that they never accumulated extraordinary wealth from their careers. Wally worked in the auto industry. Glenda spent many years as a maths teacher and later as a tutor. Their financial context was the very reason they had enough money to retire – they lived within it. In the same way, if you live within your means and make wise decisions, you too have the potential to reach multimillionaire status. That's the power of careful investing, compound interest and sound financial advice.

Perhaps you find yourself in need of some advice. Many who learn the five financial planning success secrets feel overwhelmed. This is perfectly natural. People who receive proper advice and professional counselling from financial advisers fare better than those who don't. While there are fees associated with professional financial planning, they provide a worthwhile return on investment. A relationship with a financial planner offers somebody to answer questions and coach you along the way.

Let's say you're thinking of speaking with a certified financial planner. What can you expect? At Fisher Dugmore Group, our first conversation is devoted to understanding what makes you tick. How you feel about money. What's going on in your personal life. The money goals that you have. Your appetite for risk. There is no same-size-fits-all plan. Your unique answers will shape your unique plan. That said, any wise financial plan will mirror your ideal lifestyle, not the other way around.

Once we know your financial priorities, we gather information on your income, expenses, assets and liabilities. We then perform a financial analysis to see where you currently are so that we can recommend an investment risk strategy, short- and long-term investments and savings goals for children's education and other personal objectives that you want to achieve. All these are tailor-made for your situation, whether that be to stabilise your current situation, keep a strong ship afloat, propel you to achieve bigger goals or a combination of all three.

Simply put, our financial planning relationship will allow you to use everything at your disposal to its fullest. You might not be exactly where you want to be, and that's perfectly fine. The day I wrote this chapter, I met with a client who had lost a lot of money during the 2008 global recession. That's when he reached out to ask me to take over his portfolio, and I happily obliged. Today, this man and his wife are exactly where they want to be, in terms of both financial security and disposable income. This allows them to fulfil bucket-list wishes long before retirement.

You don't need to do anything before reaching out to a certified financial planner. You don't need to have your income, expenses, assets and liabilities all neatly documented (although it does speed up the process). You don't even need to have started saving. If you're discouraged about your situation, know that it isn't permanent. The future is not equal to the past. Change is possible regardless of present circumstances. However, what you do need is the right attitude. You must realise that change is needed and you must *want* to change and follow through. If you decide to apply the strategies in this book on your own without the help of a financial planner, you'll find that all the effort you put into changing your context and circumstances is worth it. This I guarantee.

As you continue your journey towards Destination Wealth, carry with you this reminder: there are no right or wrong decisions. What matters is perfect alignment. What matters is being content with where you are, being comfortable with what you have and living within your new context. Your success and that of the generations to come depend on it. This is the greatest success secret of all: at the end of the day, your financial success is for more than just you. Your success is for your family, your loved ones, your community and your country.

This past Christmas holiday season, I took my family on a cruise. While my boys and I gazed out over the pure blue waters of the Caribbean Sea, I spoke to them.

"This trip symbolises everything I've achieved," I said. "And everything I can give you. But I will know that I truly succeeded when you can give the same or better to your children. And it's not even about the money," I added. "It's knowing that you're able to find your spot in the world and live with a sense of purpose."

May you find your spot in the world and live with a sense of purpose in the years ahead. Thank you for joining me on this journey. I have all the gratitude in the world for the time you invested in reading this book and putting its lessons in place. I look forward to celebrating your success as the work of my mind, my hands and my heart – this book – brings you to Destination Wealth!

About the Author

DAVE FISHER IS A Certified Financial Planner (CFP) ® having obtained a postgraduate as well as an advanced postgraduate diploma in financial planning (UFS).

His more than thirty years of industry experience, together with a passion for success coaching and helping others grow their financial context, enable him to follow a unique life and financial planning process with clients. Learn more at www.fisherdugmore.co.za.